D1244006

The SINGER-SONGWRITER'S Guide to RECORDING in the HOME STUDIO

SHANE ADAMS

To Robert Nyle Adams, the greatest of all.

BERKLEE PRESS

Editor in Chief: Jonathan Feist
Senior Vice President of Online Learning and Continuing Education/CEO of Berklee Online: Debbie Cavalier
Assistant Vice President of Marketing and Recruitment for Berklee Online: Mike King
Dean of Continuing Education: Carin Nuernberg
Editorial Assistants: Reilly Garrett, Emily Jones, Eloise Kelsey
Photos by Shane Adams (unless otherwise indicated)
Cover by Arnel Gregorio
Cover Photographers: Jonathan Feist (Top, featuring Lauren Marx), Joshua Resnick (Bottom)

ISBN 978-0-87639-171-6

DISTRIBUTED BY

Berklee Online

online.berklee.edu

HAL•LEONARD®
CORPORATION
7777 W. BLUEMOUND RD. P.O. BOX 13819
MILWAUKEE, WISCONSIN 53213

1140 Boylston Street
Boston, MA 02215-3693 USA
(617) 747-2146
Visit Berklee Press Online at
www.berkleepress.com

Visit Hal Leonard Online
www.halleonard.com

CONTENTS

ACKNOWLEDGMENTS vi

INTRODUCTION: THE MODERN SONGWRITER'S STUDIO ix

CHAPTER 1. HOME STUDIO SETUP AND GEAR 1

    Computer 2

        External Hard Drive 2

    Recording Software: Digital Audio Workstations 3

    Microphone 5

    Audio Interface 5

    Headphones 6

    Monitors/Speakers 8

    The Room 11

        Noise Control 15

    Minor Gear 15

        Portable Recording Devices 15

        Wi-Fi 16

    Cables 17

        Organizing Cables 18

    Microphone Stands 19

    Pop Filters 19

    Mic Pads 20

    Direct Injection Boxes 21

    Electricity Control 22

CHAPTER 2. THE RECORDING PROCESS 25

    Using Your Home Studio 25

    Set Up and Go! 25

    Creating a Mixdown 28

    Troubleshooting Your Audio Setup 29

    Stages of Recording 30

    Preproduction 30

        Designing Your Personal Sonic Landscape 30

        Which Song to Record 31

        Setting a Schedule 31

        How Much Time It Takes to Record 31

        Giving Musicians What They Need 32

    Production 33

        Finding the Right Tempo 33

        Finding the Right Key 34

    Tracking Strategies 35

        Full Bands vs. One Player at a Time 36

        Click Tracks 36

        Producing Other Singer-Songwriters 37

        Getting Great Performances 39

Postproduction 40
    Mixing 40
    Mastering 41
The Home-Studio Production Mindset 42

CHAPTER 3. RECORDING LIVE PLAYERS **45**
Setting Up a Tracking Session 45
    Signal Level 46
    Instrument Settings for Optimum Recording 47
    Correcting Phase 47
Types of Microphones 48
    Microphone Patterns 49
Auditioning Microphones 51
Recording Vocals 51
    Isolating Vocals 53
Recording Guitar 53
    Acoustic Guitar 54
    Electric Guitar 55
    Bass Guitar 58
Recording Keyboards 59
    Keyboard Audio 60
    Keyboard with MIDI 60
    Acoustic Piano 61
Recording Drums 62
    Virtual Drums 63
Recording Other Acoustic Instruments 64
Know Your Room 64

CHAPTER 4. DAW SESSION MANAGEMENT **66**
Recording Templates 67
Click Tracks 68
Take Sheet 69
Busses 69
Headphone Mixes 70
Submixes 72
Track Documentation 73
Keyboard Shortcuts 74

CHAPTER 5. MIDI AND VIRTUAL INSTRUMENTS **76**
MIDI Loops 77
Real-Time vs. Step-Time Recording 77
Buying MIDI Files 79
Virtual Instrument Setup 80
MIDI Hardware 81
Synthesizers and Samplers 83

CHAPTER 6. USING LOOPS IN THE CREATIVE SONGWRITING PROCESS **85**
MIDI Loops 87
Audio Drum Loops 88
Where to Find Loops 88
Working with Loops 91

Auditioning Loops. 93

Loops in Templates 93

Layering Loops. 95

Other Loop Generators. 95

Arpeggiators 95

Arranger Keyboards 96

Software Loop Generators 97

A Final Thought About Loops. 97

CHAPTER 7. EDITING **98**

Cutting and Pasting Tracks. 98

Volume Automation 98

Comping Tracks 100

Track Documentation. 101

Overdubbing. 101

Overdubbing over Rhythm Tracks 101

Overdubbing Multiple Takes 102

Overdubbing for Corrections: Punching In and Out 105

Editing Stray Sounds 105

Pitch Correction. 106

Fixing Timing 107

Crossfades 107

Arranging During Mixing 108

CHAPTER 8. MIXING **109**

Frequency Range 110

Panning 113

Adding Plug-Ins 114

Depth of Field. 115

Reverb vs. Delay. 116

Compression. 117

Grouping Tracks. 118

Order of Events. 118

Localized Adjustments. 118

Reference Tracks 119

CHAPTER 9. FINAL STEPS: MASTERING AND MORE **120**

Tools of Mastering. 121

EQ and Compression 121

Loudness 122

Mastering Software. 122

Mastering Speakers. 123

Song Order. 123

Hiring a Mastering Engineer 124

AFTERWORD. **125**

ABOUT THE AUTHOR **126**

INDEX. **127**

ACKNOWLEDGMENTS

I am indebted to the following:

- Jonathan Feist, my editor and co-conspirator. This project would not exist without your confidence, guidance, and graceful endurance of duress. I admire you on too many levels to mention here. I am superfluously grateful for your friendship and apple knowledge.

- Donna Hague (my sixth grade elementary school teacher!), you were the first to believe in my potential and the first to plant the seed that I could write a book.

- Cheryl Syphus, the repercussions of your gentle and loving guidance towards a barely making it, scatterbrained, High School English ruffian, are still being felt today. You gave me a chance when no others would. I am truly in your debt.

- Robert Ball, the amazing musician and musical father figure who showed me the North Star and gave me my bearings.

- Buddy Hill, I tried your patience in your piano studio. You made the piano matter to me.

- Kathleen Flake, dearest of friends.

- Kenny Varga (KV67), my Nashville brother, chief musical collaborator, friend, ear, and musical twin. I feel like you are half of my brain—the better half. You have enriched my life in incomprehensible ways.

- Eric Price, my confidant and brother. The only musician I can truly read without thinking.

- Tony Lefler, my oldest friend on Earth. Our musical dreams as young boys led me here. The foundation of who I am reaches deep into the roots of our friendship.

- Keith Sandin, I admire you more than I can express. I am a better person because of your friendship.

- The Mahaffey family, the humor and love I experienced within the walls of your home are a permanent part of my being.

- Jesse Curtis, the smartest human being I know. Too many adventures to count...your friendship is the world to me.

- Rodney Greene, my faithful friend and chief midnight-long-talk-at-the-buffet companion.

- Kurt Thompson, cohort and leader of shenanigans. You are my model of success.

- Roger King Jr., you fearlessly harbor my deepest secrets and highest joys. You are the definition of friend.

- Mark Hardt, my unexpected bonus Boston brother. You embody the qualities of the consummate professional I desire to be.

- Rodney Williams, your spark and infectious drive continuously inspire me to be better.

- Ben Klinger, you opened the world of recording to me. You gave me my first session and have since remained a bright star in the constellation of my closest friends.

- Jan Stolpe, you started my production journey and engaged my love of gear. Your friendship, professionally and personally, is one of the hallmarks of my life.

- Rob Gonzalez, one of the most gifted musicians I have ever met. You were a star when we met, and remain brighter so today. Giving me Durgin Park changed the trajectory of my musical life.

- Frank DeBretti, by far, the most brilliant musician I have ever encountered. You are the pinnacle.

- Tim Denbo, your talent continually astounds and inspires me. You have never given anything less than amazing.

- Johnny Rabb, you are the result of some sort of mad science experiment that combined tenacity, talent, decency, and humor.

- Bobby Stanton, your instruction laid the foundation for so much of what I do professionally. I am indebted to you.

- Pat Pattison, my mentor above all other mentors. I owe you my musical career.

- Jimmy Kachulis, I bow to your vast knowledge and infectious love of songwriting. The gracious weight of your legacy informs all I do.

- Justin McNaughton, you are the thoughtful, level headed, and (amazingly) astute friend/partner I do not deserve.

- Tyler Castleton, you have my utmost respect and deepest affection, my friend. In every way you are two steps above your peers.

- Rich Parkinson, you are an unflagging reminder to work hard and stay true to your principles.

- Toni Maisano Ross, Gayle Quailey, and Creson Jones, I try every day to emulate your example of gracious leadership and enduring kindness to others.

- Leanne Segura, my biggest cheerleader and humblest supporter. I am a better man because of our friendship.

- Warren White, who allowed me to grow and expand my technical knowledge at Pro Audio Solutions. You remain a great teacher and friend.

- Wilber Schaeffer, Kim Barclay Ritzer, Jeff Tidwell, Shannon Shogren, my adopted *Bonanza* family. You are the epitome of talent and friendship.

- Deborah Owens, inspiration, muse, part Selene, part Euterpe, part Steena.

- Johnny London, sacred geometry! You remain inspiring!

- Clay Essig, my film brother. You're an example of bravery and perseverance.

- Much love and respect to my VIP tribe. I am honored to be part of your family. Please add "and especially" before each of your names! Dave and Shannon Stroud, Ingrid Schnell, Mindy Pack, Lisa Haupert, Wendy Parr, Gregg Consentino, Kelly Farrell, Camiah Mingorance, Line Hilton, Ian Davidson, Darcy Deutsch, Stephanie Bare, Steve Giles, Nicole Larsen, Chris Johnson, Whitney Nichole Cytryn, Juri Tiara, Eddie Robson, Karen Moondragon, Kyle Martin, Joshua Alamu, Tersila Romero, John Henny, Joy Fields, Nara Boone, Kaya Carney, Tom Harrison, Sheena Ladwa, Jewels Jaselle, Denosh Bennett, the Peros family, Iari Melchor, Dahlia Lagos, Karen Titze Cox, John-Mark Seltzer, Erin Reagan, and Chrissy Rogers. (I know I'm leaving many out . . . forgive!)

- Mike O'Rear, a true icon of Music Row. It was an honor working for you. I learned so much in your office and in your presence.

- To my friends and family at the Country Music Hall of Fame and Museum: Ali Tonn, Nathalie Lavine, David Bogart, Danie Herbst, and Kelley Jones Luberecki. I am humbled by your awesomeness.

- Tammy Bondurant, I am indebted to your timeless love and support.

- Josh Preston, you are who I want to be when I grow up. You are a true music industry renaissance man. I am grateful for your friendship (and Lisa rocks!).

- Michael Hinckley, I am proud to be your producer, and prouder to be your friend. You are a musical inspiration to me.

- Carin Nuernberg, you are so amazing to me. I am grateful for your friendship, support, and leadership at Berklee Online. The world is a better place because you are in it.

- My Berklee and private students: your unfailing creativity and verve inspire me.

- Maura-Lee Albert, I am grateful for your patience. There is no better mother on Earth.

- Maurgea, Evangelia, and Isadora: There is no father alive more proud, and more captivated by the brilliant light and love of his beautiful daughters than I. I love you to the moon, the stars, the sun, and back (don't forget the whole world).

The Modern Songwriter's Studio

There are a number of factors in today's music industry that have contributed to the rise of the home studio. Most obviously, recording technology to let average musicians record and release their own music has become affordable, easy to use, and exceptionally high quality. If you have a computer, you only need a few hundred more dollars to be able to make recordings at a quality level that could have cost millions of dollars to produce only a few decades ago.

Other factors are also driving the need for home studios. The industry model is shifting away from artists being signed by major record labels, in favor of them producing their recordings independently. The advents of close fan contact via social media and of audio streaming have put more emphasis on artists producing singles, rather than albums. So, we are frequently releasing singles, rather than working on larger albums, and the former economy of scale that could come from using a commercial studio space is no longer driving our patterns of writing and releasing songs.

Artists at all levels are finding the need to have their own home studios, even if they only use them for scratch recordings and still do their final work in commercial spaces. But many artists are no longer finding the need to use a commercial studio.

For many years, I have been consulting to songwriters in Nashville and around the country about how to develop their own studios. Sometimes, these are stand-alone commercial spaces, but more often in the artists' homes. Many of my clients are new to the recording process. But some are very experienced. For example, I've been working with Byron Gallimore, the GRAMMY®-winning producer for Faith Hill, Tim McGraw, and many others, on putting together a home studio to make quick demos—actually, in one of his big, walk-in closets. He then brings his artists to world-class commercial studios. On the other end of the spectrum, I work with many songwriters who are just getting into it, and simply want to be able to have an affordable way to record their music and get it out there.

Personally, for the artists I produce, we tend to record in our home studios, and then send our tracks to dedicated mixing and mastering engineers. While we can certainly do these tasks in our home studios, there are benefits to simply having fresh ears and greater experience managing these phases of the projects, so I try to bring in other engineers when the budget allows. Mastering studios, in particular, tend to have gear that is superior to what is affordable to the rest of us. While a home mastering job will typically focus only on adjusting loudness, a mastering engineer can also fine tune the track's overall sound and make it sound a lot more pleasing, and doing this well requires a lot of training and experience. It's possible to get it pretty close in a home studio, but I personally feel that you can get better quality by having specialists handle the mixing and mastering. There is also a great benefit in having someone with fresh ears make final, subtle adjustments at the end of the process.

So, there are different ways that people set up, use, and integrate these spaces into their processes.

Typically, my clients seek me out after investing a fair amount of time on their own, trying to get it all to work. A common experience is that they go to one of the big gear retailers and get sold a bunch of gear that is unnecessary or inappropriate for their needs: the wrong kinds of mics, or interfaces, or software that they don't know how to use. They waste a considerable amount of time trying to figure it all out, and then eventually, realize that they are in over their heads.

In this book, I will share some of the common advice and techniques that they find most helpful, and that finally leads them to getting the full benefit from having their own recording capabilities.

And those benefits are very significant. With today's technology, an artist with only passable technological aptitude can create a recording that is at a very professional level—that's "good enough" for most intents and purposes. Of course, there are benefits to engaging professional engineers for tracking, mixing, and mastering. A world-class room has practical benefits. For some projects, it is worth going into a commercial studio. There, you will be able to record more instruments simultaneously, have access to more gear options that would be impossible for most individuals to afford, and benefit by a team of experts who will adeptly handle tasks of making nuanced adjustments to sound quality, not to mention running out and getting doughnuts for the band, should they require more of them.

On the other hand, when you record in your own facility and on your own time, you have the luxury to try as many takes as you like. You are free from the pressure of others waiting for you, or watching you, or judging what you are doing. You might have some sonically interesting spaces in your home that are different from the carefully calibrated studio space: the reverberation in your bathroom, the complete deadness of your coat closet, the semi-live balance of your living room. You can record spontaneously, as the spirit moves you, rather than when the studio is available. And you can easily make quick, scratch recordings to informally send around to your cowriters, bandmates, manager, or friends, to get some feedback, and have something inexpensive to produce and nimble to revise. While it's nice to have a trained engineer run the show, the tools have become simple enough to use that many artists can perform the required tasks themselves. Particularly now that most high end DAWs let you control the essential tasks from your iPhone or other device, the need for a separate control room and a dedicated tracking engineer in a home studio is often unnecessary.

If you get appropriate gear and learn to use it effectively, as we'll discuss in this book, your home studio can give you very high quality professional recordings. While a full service commercial studio might ultimately yield you a slicker result, in many cases, my rule of thumb is that most home studios can get you about 80 percent there. And most of the time, for most artists, that is good enough. Most listeners can't tell whether a recording is made in someone's living room or in a commercial studio. We generally only need to go to commercial recording studios when larger ensembles need to record simultaneously.

In this book, my goal isn't to teach you to become a professional engineer. Rather, I want to give you the tools to set up a home studio and use it to make decent quality recordings. I will recommend some of my favorite gear, which has been tested many times by many different clients, at all echelons of the music industry. Of course, new products are always coming on the market, so I'll mostly stick with reputable brands that have been around for a while, more than individual models.

We songwriters want to get our songs heard. That's the ultimate goal: to share our music with an audience, and to have our recordings reach the widest possible audience. These are recordings at the highest level. In addition, we use recordings to send our songs to publishers, to clubs where we're hoping to get gigs, and we even send individual tracks for use on other people's projects. Many bands today exist virtually, and it's commonplace now for everyone involved on a recording to record their parts in their own home studios and then send files to someone who will then knit them all together. And we'll even use recording gear to simply capture or archive our ideas, for later use or refinement, as part of our creative process.

Being able to create decent quality recordings has become one of the expected, core skills of contemporary musicians of all types, from drummers to piano players to producers. Recording instrumental parts for other people's songs has become a common way for musicians to create income. Everyone can produce their parts at their own pace, in the privacy of their own homes, and perform as many takes as they like in order to get a final result that they feel is their best work, without holding up the rest of the band. Some will do it in one take, others will do it in fifty takes, all without the pressure of producing their tracks in front of everyone else, in a studio environment. You can edit and tune your track days later, without having to schedule additional studio time for overdubs. You can experiment and try radically different approaches to creating a part, and listen to them without anybody else witnessing it or paying for studio time. And nobody involved in a home-recorded endeavor has to pay for parking, for cartage, or for babysitting. They don't have to show up at the same time. All that matters is their ability to eventually produce a track that sounds amazing.

Songwriters particularly need to have these skills, and in this book, I'll discuss how to set up and use a studio specifically from a songwriter's perspective. I hope that it helps you to create some great new music!

CHAPTER 1

Home Studio Setup and Gear

In this chapter, we will talk about how to outfit your home recording studio. You may call it a project studio, a demo studio, a home studio, or something else. We'll discuss the most critical gear you'll need to outfit it to create pro-quality recordings.

In a most basic form, a serviceable home studio can begin with a laptop equipped with recording software, a good microphone, and a set of pro level headphones.

FIG. 1.1. A Minimal Studio

You can produce decent recordings with even this bare-bones, minimal setup. By expanding this configuration, you can achieve even higher quality results and have more flexibility to boot.

Aside from the gear types discussed in this chapter, I'll also give some of my personal preferences for specific products. As always, new options are always coming into the market, but if you stick with my suggestions, you'll have a good start. You can certainly add to this setup, and throughout the book, I will discuss additional possibilities.

COMPUTER

Central to a home studio is a computer. It houses your recording software (called a Digital Audio Workstation or "DAW") and stores the recordings. A big "commercial" studio will typically have a large console (or "desk"), operated with physical knobs, switches, and faders, capable of accepting a great number of microphone inputs and supporting dedicated outboard gear for sound processing. Most home studios are based around a laptop, operated with a mouse, and with sound processing all contained "in the box" (i.e., in the computer, accomplished with software).

People usually under-buy when it comes to their computer, and the biggest negative result is greater *latency*—a delay between when a sound is performed and when you hear it in your speakers. Latency is very distracting during the recording process. What's critical is to get something that has a FireWire port, as well as a USB port. It can be a laptop. A desktop machine will give you more ports, but I'm seeing fewer and fewer people using those.

Both Macs and PCs are fine for recording audio. Get whichever one you prefer.

It's amazing how much you can do with laptops these days, and they are completely portable. Until recently, you would have needed a professional studio to do what's possible on a laptop today, but that's no longer the case.

Personally, I like the MacBook Pro. You can certainly use a Windows machine, but I find that Macs have fewer problems and are easier to figure out. Get as fast a processor and as much RAM as you can—at least 8 GB of RAM. That much RAM should give your computer enough headroom to run your audio programs.

I like to have as large a screen as I can. You need enough space to edit and record your audio. A smaller screen will be more easily portable and fit into a smaller backpack. But when you are recording audio, you need to see a lot of information. The bigger the screen, the more information you can look at. Screen size, however, will always remain a personal choice. You can also get an external monitor, so that you have both that portable-size laptop and also enough screen space for serious editing.

External Hard Drive

Another recommendation I have is to utilize at least two hard drives: a system hard drive, where you keep all of your program information, and an audio hard drive where you keep your audio files. It is not good to keep your audio files on your system hard drive. Your system will run more efficiently if your DAW program is on your system drive. Also, if your system drive crashes, you won't lose any of your audio files, or any of your projects, because they will be stored on your audio hard drive. Keep them separate. You'll thank me later.

Storing your audio files on a separate external drive also saves CPU resources and reduces latency issues, so that you are hearing what you are performing in real time.

Some hard drives are "solid state." Solid-state drives make no noise because they have no moving parts. However, they are usually much more expensive and have lower storage capacities than traditional drives. Traditional hard drives consist of a spinning internal disc that houses your stored information. They can be noisy but they are also less expensive and come in a wide variety of large storage capacities.

Make sure you get an external drive that has at least a 7,200 rotational rate, rather than 5,200. I like Seagate drives. Spending a little extra on a robust hard drive really helps. One of the most common catastrophic problems that can bring down a studio is hard drive failure, so get a high quality one. I recommend using a medium-sized system drive (today, that means around 500 GB) and then a larger external drive for your files (500 to 750 GB). Hard drive prices are pretty cheap, so it won't hurt you to get something larger than 750 GB. However, rather than something enormous, I also recommend using multiple smaller hard drives. This way, you lessen the possibility of losing too much information.

Related to hard drives is backup. Gobbler is a service designed to archive audio sessions and transfer files. With most file transfer services, when you upload files to them, the files get compressed, and there is the potential for a reduction in quality. Similarly, if you Zip a file, there may be a loss of fidelity. Gobbler doesn't compress files, so the integrity of the data is protected.

RECORDING SOFTWARE: DIGITAL AUDIO WORKSTATIONS

For many years, home studios had dedicated recorders, such as 4-, 8-, or 16-track tape machines or digital recorders. But today's DAWs are much more powerful. They offer limitless tracks, editing tools, and high quality sound processing gear, not to mention built-in sounds and loops. They are easier, cheaper, and more powerful than any of the recording tools before them, and many of the same tools are now used in home and commercial studios alike.

Macs often come bundled with GarageBand, which is a simple but very useful DAW. You can record multiple tracks, apply basic processing, and use many built-in sounds and loops. Tons of commercial recordings have been created using GarageBand. Rihanna's hit "Umbrella" used a GarageBand loop. A big step up, at approximately $80, is Steinberg's Sequel, which you can loop with, transpose, and perform other more sophisticated tasks. It is GarageBand on steroids! Sequel is a great value, and comes bundled with over 5,000 loops. Later in this book, we'll discuss how loops can play an important part in today's songwriter studios.

While those two simple programs are useful, they have their limitations, and if your budget moves up a few hundred dollars, you can get into the realm of professional-level DAWs. These give you much higher quality sound processing capabilities. The biggest three contenders today are Cubase, Logic, and Pro Tools, and there are spirited debates regarding which one is the best. Personally, I like Cubase. It's easy to use, its VST (Virtual Studio Technology) instrument integration works beautifully (for great sounds), and it utilizes plug-ins really well. Logic is also a fantastic program, with many great sounding instruments and useful loops and sounds, and it is excellent for both audio and MIDI. Pro Tools is ubiquitous in recording studios everywhere, and it has been around forever. Common thoughts about it are that it is optimized for straight recording, but MIDI isn't supported as well as it is in other products.

I train people in all three platforms, and I know them all really well. Generally speaking, I find that Cubase lets songwriters do what they want in the fewest number of steps.

While you can buy hardware sound processing gear, the DAWs all come with high quality built-in reverb, compression, equalizers, delay, and other tools as plug-ins. You can buy better or more specialized ones, if you like, and there can be some performance advantages to having outboard gear. But most people with home studios don't find the need for external sound processing hardware—particularly, not at first. You can do most of it inside the box.

FIG. 1.2. Rack of Hardware Outboard Gear

MICROPHONE

You need at least one excellent quality microphone, probably a condenser microphone. A company I like that has affordable, excellent microphones is Avantone. Medium end, I like Audio-Technica. We'll talk more about microphones in chapter 3.

A minimal microphone setup can be attained by using a USB microphone plugged into your computer. Ideally, choose a regular condenser microphone for your recording.

AUDIO INTERFACE

An audio interface is the device that links your microphones and monitors (speakers) to your computer. It can connect to your computer via USB or FireWire.

The audio interface is the heart of your rig. Choosing a good audio interface can make all the difference in your recording. They come in many shapes and sizes. Hundreds of interfaces are available, varying greatly both in the quantity of ports they have and their quality level.

There are several reasons why you need an audio interface. First, the audio card that comes inside your computer was designed more for audio playback, rather than processing the huge audio files of a recording project. When you throw big audio files through a native audio card, your computer will most likely perform very, very slowly. A slow computer adds audio ticks, pops, and other forms of unremovable digital distortion to your audio track.

Audio interfaces take the audio processing away from your computer's card and runs the audio for it. They are built to withstand a tremendous amount of audio information.

More reasons to have an audio interface are that you can record more than one microphone simultaneously, and you can have multiple options to play your audio back—through multiple headphone jacks, multiple speakers, etc.

The first question to ask when purchasing an audio interface is, "How many parts do I need to record at the same time?" Audio interfaces range from one input to many inputs. Get an audio interface that has enough inputs for your recording needs.

A common mistake my clients make before coming to me is that they purchase an audio interface that doesn't have enough input ports. For example, if you are playing guitar and singing, you may only need two inputs. If you are a duo, and you and your partner want to record guitars and vocals at the same time, you'll need at least four inputs. If you want to also record a MIDI keyboard, or a drum set, or simultaneously record your whole band at once, you'll need something bigger—say, sixteen inputs. Most audio interfaces have a least two mic inputs and outputs for a pair of studio speakers.

Another advantage of using an audio interface is its robustness—its processing power and buffering speed, which affect how it interacts with a computer. Under-performing interfaces introduce latency to the recording process. While you might be able to reduce the latency a little bit with your software, the computer eventually won't be able to handle it, so you inevitably wind up with skipping beats, dropping voices, buzzing, or other digital artifacts. This is a very common result of cheap interfaces.

Typically, buying a large interface with lots of inputs does not give you better quality than the smaller interfaces with a few inputs. Different companies usually use the same processing chip in their small and large interfaces. Across a product line, the difference is usually in how many inputs they offer.

I'm a great fan of RME audio interfaces, which are high quality. If you're on a tighter budget, Focusrite has some nice entry level interfaces, such as the Saffire series.

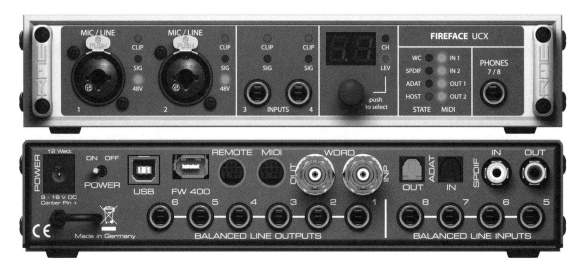

FIG. 1.3. RME Audio Interface. Photo courtesy of RME.

HEADPHONES

Headphones are used:

- by musicians when they record, so that they can hear the other tracks
- by the recording engineer to hear what's being recorded, and
- by the mixing engineer as another point of reference for how the tracks sound all together.

In commercial studios, engineers work in separate soundproof control rooms, which permit them to listen to what is being recorded without that sound bleeding into the microphones. Home studio engineers rely on headphones for that purpose.

Ideally, you'll use external monitors for listening back to your music. But starting out, you can get away with high quality headphones.

For recording, you should get "over-the-ears" headphones. These have foam cups, looking like little toilet seats that fit over your ears.

An issue with headphones is how much they bleed into the mics. If you have a singer singing, and they have the click track very loud, or their mix is very loud in their headphones, that sound can actually bleed into the vocal track. Some singers will sing with only one of the headphone cups over their ears, which exposes the other one to the microphone. Those are just things that you have to deal with, with headphones.

I personally use Sennheiser, as I find that some other brands accentuate certain frequencies too much, often sounding bass heavy. AKG and Sony make good headphones too. A decent set of studio headphones will cost anywhere from about $50 to $125.

FIG. 1.4. Sennheiser Headphones HD 280 Pro. Photo courtesy of Sennheiser Electronic Corporation.

If you're just recording guitar or bass, or instruments such as keyboards that aren't necessarily recording into a microphone, you might get away with a cheaper brand of headphones, because you're not in danger of audio bleed from them. But definitely for vocals, you'll need a better set of headphones.

MONITORS/SPEAKERS

Though you could listen back to your work using headphones, you'll get a much more realistic sense of your recordings if you use studio monitors. These also connect to an audio interface, which might be able to play back through several different sets of monitors.

There's a difference between studio monitors and home stereo speakers. Home speakers are typically optimized (EQ'd) to make the sound seem better. They typically boost the signal's high end and low signals, because this makes the overall sound more pleasing to most people. With a studio monitor, you're not going for a pleasing sound; you want to have accuracy of sound so that you know where the different elements (voice, guitar, bass, drums, etc.) sit in the mix. It should have a flat response across the frequency spectrum.

When you're mixing, you're dealing with three dimensions of space:

1. left and right, or "panning"
2. vertical up and down, the "frequencies," with low frequencies being on the bottom and high frequencies being on top
3. spacial depth, or "reverb"—the 3-D effect.

A good studio monitor will represent those three fields. When you're mixing, it's almost like you want to hear how *bad* your mix is. Once you can get it sounding good on a set of studio monitors, it will sound great on a car stereo, or your home speaker system, your computer speakers, headphones, or other consumer products.

The perfect placement for studio monitors is to have them spaced like an equilateral triangle between your head and the speakers. You want the sound coming at you at the same time, so you want to be in the sweet spot, where the sound of the speakers arrive at your ears simultaneously. So, at your workspace, measure your head to the speakers and the speakers to each other. On most speakers, there are a woofer (lower frequencies) and tweeter (higher). If you must lay them on their sides, keep the woofers closer to the center. When you mix, a common technique is to start with your lower frequencies towards the center—bass drums, bass guitar— and higher frequencies (guitars, cymbals) towards the sides.

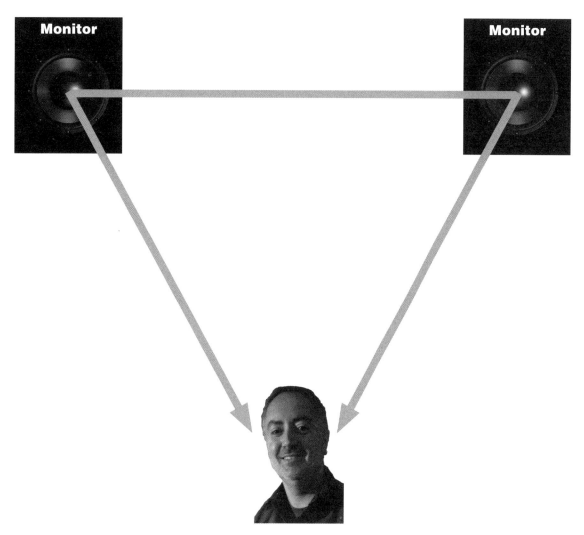

FIG. 1.5. Equidistant Between Speakers

You can buy various speaker stands. For example, in my own studio, I keep my speakers tipped towards me via special stands designed for the purpose.

There are various types of monitors—for example, near field, mid field, and far field. Those are general directions for how far away the speakers will be placed from you. I really love the Dynaudio Acoustics. For a small set of speakers, they have the BM5s or BM6s, which are really nice sounding speakers. Numbers like the "5" or "6" usually refer to the woofer diameter, in inches. I recommend at least a 6-inch woofer diameter; an 8-inch diameter would be better. The larger sizes increase the amount of frequencies you can hear while you're mixing.

People argue about what their favorite speakers are: KRK, Genelec, JBL, etc. A cheap solution is Behringer, which, for speakers, are good quality and inexpensive.

Ideally, you will augment the speakers with a subwoofer—not to have banging bass so that you can annoy your neighbors, but just so that you can actually hear what bass sounds are present in your recording.

Another ideal situation is to have a secondary set of speakers that are designed to mimic low quality consumer gear. The standard is Auratone (often referred to as "horror tone"). Having a nice pair of monitors and then a set of Auratones allows you to switch the sound back and forth so that you can get a sense of how the mix will sound on a variety of systems. Similarly, you might test the mix in progress on a consumer system, such as your home stereo or your car. My colleague Kenny Varga is an engineer, and we joke about listening to our mixes in "Studio C"—in our cars. Once we finish a mix on our studio monitors, we listen first in his car, then in my car, then on the computer speakers—in as many different places as we can.

It's good to find monitors on which you can mix at a lower volume. Some brands, such as KRK speakers, sound really great at louder levels, but harsh at lower volumes. In the long haul, this can lead to hurting your ears. Being able to get a balanced sound at lower volumes is physiologically healthier.

Whatever studio speakers you use, it is helpful to stick with the same brand and model. You will then get used to those speakers and learn how to mix on them. Every speaker has its idiosyncrasies, so you just have to get to know the sound of them.

I personally use a pair of Tannoys, which have a *concentric speaker*. There is an additional mid-range speaker inside the woofer, so the mid and low frequencies reach my ears at exactly the same time, even if the speakers are on their sides.

FIG. 1.6. Tannoy Studio Monitors

Active speakers have built-in amplifiers; *passive* speakers rely on external amplifiers. Active speakers are more efficient, with amplifiers designed specifically for that speaker. They are more expensive to repair, and require more specific parts. Often, they include a dipswitch EQ to let you tune the speaker to your studio environment. If you have a lot of high or low end, you can tune the speaker to get a flat response.

Passive speakers are a bit more old school, where an external amplifier powers the speakers, and the speakers just reproduce the sound.

There are ways to fine-tune your listening environment, so that you can be sure that the sound you are hearing from your monitors is typical of what the recording will sound like on a variety of systems and in a variety of rooms. Speaker companies often have proprietary software or devices you can use to measure the speaker's output level. For example, Tannoy has JBL, which is used like a spectrometer—a meter that shows a range of frequencies (like an EQ), and what's augmented or dipping in your room. It has dipswitches that let you adjust the sound to arrive at a more characteristic spectrum. For devices that don't have proprietary software, you can get the same effect using a third-party SPL meter and a spectrometer.

THE ROOM

Besides the audio and computer gear, the most critical consideration, when creating a new studio, is to decide its location. Again, your initial "home studio" might just be a laptop and a microphone. That's portable; you can move it wherever you like, and it doesn't need a permanent home. When you get more serious, though, you will want to have a more permanent, dedicated space. It's important to weigh all of your options and understand the possibilities that you may have close at hand—which are often richer than many people imagine.

Instead of going for something acoustically perfect, look for someplace comfortable. Where is it comfortable to sing, where is it comfortable to play? Is it your living room? A den? A bedroom?

There are also some quietness factors to consider. You don't want a noisy fridge humming in the background, or a gurgling fish tank, and you definitely have to watch out for an errant air conditioner kicking in. All in all these can be contained, for the most part (during your session, turn off the air/tank/fridge). Still, a great performance in a not-so-perfect room will still beat a lame performance in dead silence.

Then, consider the various acoustic properties of all the rooms at your disposal—office, living room, bedroom, closets, whatever you have. Regular box-shaped rooms can have a kind of "pinging" effect, accentuating higher frequencies. Rooms with irregular wall or ceiling shapes will have a more even sound.

Spaces with soft surroundings, such as carpeting and upholstered furniture, may sound "dead," or without reverberation. But your room doesn't have to be an anechoic/silent chamber—a trend in commercial spaces for a while, but one that most studios have moved away from. Still, though, most commercial studios tend to be relatively dead. While a dead room gives you a lot of control to develop the sound electronically, initially, the sound will be dull and lifeless unless you brighten it up with electronic processing (such as reverb).

Sounds that are naturally beautiful at the point of recording will almost certainly be more appealing than what you can create artificially—and this is actually a benefit of home studios. Recordings made in more livable spaces will often sound more natural than those created in a studio environment and then modified with a lot of sound processing tools, which will have a degrading effect after a while. Real rooms with some harder surfaces—glass windows, wood floors, and stone fireplaces—will sound more "live" and reverberant, with more distinctive overtones and richer, more natural acoustics. They might be more difficult to control, though, even with studio gear, so if there's a problem, such as too much reverb or accentuation of an undesirable frequency, it might not be possible to edit it to become what you are after.

So, while the extremes might be helpful in certain circumstances, most of the time you will want to record in a space that has the right acoustic balance. Most spaces need some tuning to become optimized for recording, managing the way it reflects and absorbs different frequencies. While there are commercial products available to help accomplish this, you can often improve a room's sound with furnishings. An "audio diffuser" can be a well-placed bookcase or a window treatment.

I try to tune the room sound by using what my clients have on hand. A home studio space also has to be livable. A songwriter's spouse will tend not to want their stuff cluttering up the house. So I try to use what is already there, rather than buying dedicated audio control products designed for changing studio acoustics. Soft, uneven surfaces such as upholstered chairs and rugs diffuse or absorb frequencies. Hard, smooth surfaces, such as pictures under glass and exposed wood, add a natural reverb.

While commercial studios generally have isolation booths, home studios tend to have less recordings going on simultaneously, and so these are not usually critical components. Achieving true isolation in a home without investing in a serious construction effort is an ideal often meandering towards the desert, if not a complete lost cause. There will probably be some bleed between microphones, in a home studio recording of a band recording simultaneously. While that can complicate editing, it is actually often beneficial for the overall sound.

Test out different rooms; you might find that some are particularly good for certain purposes. The old cliché of recording vocals in your bathroom in order to get natural reverb often actually works really well! Also try putting your guitar amp in there. That can give a nice sound. People do it all the time!

Often, getting a good sound is a matter of microphone orientation. One client I had set up a studio in his living room, which happened to be a naturally great sounding room. The way they set up their window treatments, the couch, the hardwood floors, a really interesting bookcase, and the rug—it all contributed to the room being a really nice acoustic space. Initially, we set up the microphone in front of their brick fireplace, because when he sang, it gave his voice a wonderful warmth. But when we listened to a test recording, we were surprised to find that the bass frequencies were unnaturally amplified, for some reason. Rather than change the room, we simply turned the microphone about 15 degrees to the left, and that cleared up the problem right away. It sounded great. So, many factors will contribute to a room's sound, and you have to experiment.

When I set up a room for recording in the home of a singer/songwriter client, I imagine I'm setting up an intimate "club" setting, which is the iconic sound space for that type of music. It's useful to imagine the kind of space where the artist is likely to perform. What environment is it in? A concert hall? A stadium? A small venue? A coffee house? A garage? All of those places have some common elements: features of the room that reflect sound, and features that absorb sound.

Generally, hard objects reflect sound. Walls, windows, amp stacks, wooden chairs and tables, bookcases: anything metal, wood, or plastic. Soft objects absorb sound: rugs, upholstery, curtains, cushions, textiles, and fabrics.

We don't want to eliminate these elements, we want to *balance* them—to create a good mix of reflection and absorption.

Here's where the small club idea comes into play. Imagine watching a performer on a small club stage and it sounds great. What is contributing to that sound? It's usually a wooden stage (i.e., a reflective surface), the people watching—especially the first row (absorptive: their clothes, hair), maybe small round tables (reflective), and the walls of the club (reflective). A typical small club is a 60 percent reflective and 40 percent absorptive room.

So, if that's your style, you can try to recreate that in your home studio. Do a room acoustics checklist.

What are the reflective surfaces?	What are the absorptive elements?
Hardwood floor	Cushy couch
Coffee table	Futon
Fireplace	Throw rug
Wood chairs	Full-room carpeting
Windows	Drapes
Bookcase	Dad's Barcalounger
Plasma TV	Grandma's quilt hung on a wall
China cabinet	Lampshades
Walls	Mattresses
Stairway	
End tables	
Vases	
Dining room table	
Computer desk	
Computer monitor	

FIG. 1.7. Room Acoustics Checklist

So, ask: What do you think is the reflective/absorptive percentage in the room you want to record in? Is there a way to get closer to the 60 percent reflective/40 percent absorptive percentages?

For example, let's say you want to record vocals in your medium-sized bedroom. The walls are reflective, and the bed is absorptive; those are the big elements. What about the floor? A carpeted room will probably sound more muffled, whereas a hardwood floor will sound more reflective and "live." Are there curtains? Those'll be absorptive. A dresser, mirror, headboard...all of those are reflective. What are the reflective/absorptive percentages?

Living rooms are usually the biggest room of a house/apartment. Does it have wall-to-wall carpeting? Hardwood floor? A couch? What other chairs? Bookcases? A TV? Pictures on canvas? Glass? What are the reflective/absorptive percentages?

Take an inventory of your room, compare it to the type of space that makes sense for your music's performance, and then adjust it as you can.

Noise Control

Another primary consideration for where you locate your studio is noise control.

Here's another tip for omitting extraneous noise from outside: communicate with your neighbors. On my residential street in Nashville—the city where everybody is a songwriter—*seven* of my neighbors have home studios! So, we have developed a little phone tree. When one of us has a session, we call the others so that we are sure not to mow our lawns that day. That's a lot cheaper and easier than encapsulating our houses in soundproof shells, or constructing floating floors, like commercial studios do.

Garbage trucks, lawn mowers, traffic sounds, birds chirping, squirrels chattering, children running up and down the halls—these are the hazards of home studios, and we have to work around them. If you have the option to site your studio space in a quiet and undisturbed part of the house, you will have some more flexibility about when you are able to record.

You will have noise in your home studio. It would be too expensive and impractical to completely soundproof it in the way that a commercial studio can be soundproofed, so minimizing the effects of unwanted noise in a home studio becomes an issue of management. Just think about how to minimize the bad sounds, how to make the best use of your opportunities for quiet, and accept that you will sometimes have to do extra takes because of extraneous noise.

MINOR GEAR

Portable Recording Devices

Handheld recording devices also have a place in contemporary recording, particularly for scratch recordings/work tapes to easily capture ideas. There are iPhones, iPads, Zoom recorders, and small units by Sony, Yamaha, and Steinberg. A Zoom recorder, with two microphones in a cross pattern for a stereo field, can actually sound pretty good. Beyond just their portability, there are many recording apps available for smartphones. Companies also provide mic inputs that turn those portable devices into a little portable recording console, which is pretty neat, with connectors for XLR cables (such as by Alesis, PreSonus, etc.).

These devices are handy for recording individual instruments. If you're just recording voice and guitar, you can get a pretty good sound with a simple device, rather than a whole console.

Besides the number of inputs, the major disadvantages are: the quality of microphone on a handheld unit, and the quality of mic pre-amp. The result is fine for scratch recordings, though. I find that my iPhone, when I'm doing work tapes, records surprisingly well if I'm careful not to blast out, and if I don't sing too loud. I'll often capture ideas by placing my iPhone on my piano desk, and singing and playing right into it. It actually records really well, with no outboard gear, no nothing—just the built-in microphone.

I have a multitrack app on my iPhone, and in a pinch, I could do a quick demo: play a piano part on one track, sing on another track, play guitar on another track, and do a quick mix. I would never release it commercially! But just to capture ideas, I find the quality quite good.

Some good apps are Rectools02, Fire, GarageBand (Apple), and LoopMash (Steinberg), available for smartphones and tablets. I really like LoopMash, because you create loops, and then record to those loops.

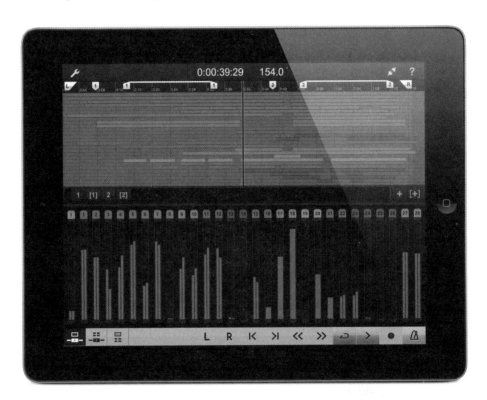

FIG. 1.8. Tablet Controls. Photo courtesy of Steinberg Media Technologies GmbH.

Wi-Fi

A wireless router for your Internet access will let you use a smartphone or tablet to control a session. The essential tasks—recording, simple editing, making new tracks, etc.—are all available. So, in my living room I have a really nice piano, and I frequently make piano-vocal recordings from there, controlling my computer with my iPhone. This isn't essential, but it is a convenient way to run a session, and because my computer is in another room, my performing environment feels like a clean, dedicated studio space.

CABLES

Audio cables connect all your gear, and it is important to have good quality cables. Usually, it's the connection point that fails on a cable—where the cable meets the actual metal connector. Good cables have strain protection close to the sleeve to keep them from bending and warping.

Plastic sleeves around the plugs indicate lower quality cables. If you're able to unscrew the connector, that's an indication of a better connector, because it's usually soldered much better. If you unscrew it and open it up, shrink-wrapped plastic sleeves over the cable usually indicate a better cable. Cables with gold-plated tips are better than steel. Noise Track and Soundcraft are two good brands of the metal pieces.

My own best cables are made by Zaolla. They are super high quality, but they're also very expensive. Quantum makes great cables. Monster makes great cables, but they're super expensive, for what they give you. You're paying a lot of money for the name more than the cable. Mogami is another really great cable; a lot of studios use those. Usually, mid-level cables will work well enough. Avoid off-market cables.

There are two types of audio cables: balanced and unbalanced. All microphone cables, with XLR rather than quarter-inch connectors, are balanced; there are three pins, for two internal wires and an outer metal grounding sheath. Quarter-inch plugs, which look like headphone jacks, come both balanced and unbalanced.

To determine whether a cable is balanced, look at the plug/connector, and note the black rings. An unbalanced cable has one black ring; a balanced cable has two black rings. On an unbalanced cable, that black ring separates the tip of the plug from the "sleeve" (or the "cylinder") of the plug. A balanced plug (two rings) is also called a "tip ring sleeve." Here, the metal sleeve of the plug is divided into two portions. Those three portions—the tip, the middle ring, and the sleeve—function exactly the same as the three little mini plugs on a microphone cable.

Balanced cables reduce hum between your instrument and the audio interface. In order for the balanced cable to function properly, the device it is plugged into has to have a balanced output. Some old, vintage synths typically do not have a balanced output, so using a balanced cable doesn't do anything. Most modern devices have balanced outputs. If it doesn't, the instrument might not operate properly, but it shouldn't hurt anything.

Organizing Cables

There are various tools for keeping cables organized. Snakes are very handy. A snake is several cables bundled together, usually manufactured in multiples of four. They are used for long runs of cable so that you don't have, say, thirty different cables on the floor.

Some snakes have plugs on each end. Some snakes end in a junction box with outputs or inputs equaling the amount of plugs on the other end. And there's another format, called DV25, which has a pin connection on one end with what looks like twenty-five holes (like a little trapezoid piece) on one end, and cable points on the other end. You can buy snakes with every imaginable combination of connections of mic cable, both the female and male versions.

Snakes typically come in eight-channel configurations, and the cables are typically color coded in the colors of a rainbow. The common order is red, orange, yellow, green, blue, violet—the old ROY G BIV configuration. Sometimes, there are also brown and black.

A really cheap, fun way to organize cables is by using different colors of plastic cable ties ("Zip ties"). When I have a stereo pair of cables, I use red and white: red for right, and white for left. I will also put one, two, three, or four on the tip to indicate the number one, two, three, or four. So my first cable will have one cable tie, the second cable will have two, third will have three, the fourth will have four, etc. That's kind of a cheap way of identifying cables. I find that labels typically fall off, at some point.

A more advanced way to identify cables is to get numbered, heat shrunk, plastic sleeves you can put on the cable, and with a blow dryer shrink them. I've done that for some studios. But the cable tie thing works really well. Put the same colored tie at each end of the cable.

Ideally, keep your cable lengths as short as possible. Fifty feet is a good max, but I know some cable runs that had to be a hundred feet or so. Longer cables essentially act as antennae, picking up audio frequencies and hum. That can be a big problem.

Similarly, try to keep your electrical cords separate from your audio cables as much as you can, because the audio cables will pick up even minute hum that occurs in an electrical cable.

Cable ties have always been a great savior of mine, I use them a lot.

You can also buy cable organizers—long tubes with a line cut in them, useful for long runs. To make my own, I've purchased four-inch rubber hoses from Home Depot, and run cables through those.

I've seen tons of effective makeshift cable organizers. I attached a plastic gutter (like to collect rain on a roof) to the back of my audio desk to keep cables off the floor. There are also various cable management systems that you can find at the local hardware store. There are flat tubes that you can run along your floor, or up a wall. A lot of people use them to hide the cables of their flat screen TV, but you can buy them in six- and eight-foot lengths if you have a long run.

Keep your cables out of the way. By wrapping them up and putting them together, you avoid how much dust will collect, which can be gross, and also, can damage your audio interface or computer.

I like to keep different lengths of my microphone cables. And I would err on the side of buying better cables—Mogami or Zaolla cables, if you can afford them. Good cables do make a difference in your studio's sound.

MICROPHONE STANDS

Having a good microphone stand really makes a tremendous difference because you're able to place the mic correctly, and cleanly, with little hassle. People often start by getting the cheapest possible microphone stands, but I always recommend getting something better.

There are two common mic stands. A simple stand consists of an upright pole as the primary mic support, with a tripod or weighted circular base. They are good for vocal mics, often used on stage. More versatile is a "boom stand." The boom is another pole that you set at an angle to the primary support. A boom increases your ability to position the mic squarely where you want it. Booms come in different sizes and counter-weighted booms. Tall stands with 6-foot long booms can reach over a drum riser. There are also shorter versions, for more general use.

The company Triad-Orbit makes amazing microphone stands, with a piston driver and articulated feet so that you can lean the microphone at an angle without using a boom stand; the boom arms are on a ball and pivot kind of assembly. So, you don't have to mess with those stupid little screw-in knobs that you can either never get tight enough, or that get so tight that you can't undo them.

Suspension cages are microphone holders or clips that utilize some kind of elastic or elastic rope material. Their purpose is to dampen any vibrations in the floor. Let's say a truck is driving by outside your studio. The rumble of that truck can carry through the floor of your house, or your room, or your studio, up through the base of the microphone stand and into the microphone. Suspending the mic in one of these microphone holders can eliminate that rumble problem. Many microphones come with some kind of suspension system.

POP FILTERS

Pop filters are particularly useful when you're recording vocals. Singing *plosives*—hard consonants like "p's" and "t's" and "d's"—can cause a level spike in your recording. Pop filters help diffuse and manage those a little better. Some studios actually use two pop filters just to be safe.

There's a great debate on what kind of pop filters to use. There are *textile* pop filters, which have a kind of a pantyhose type covering. There are also *deflection* pop filters, with metal grates that are louvered at an angle, diffusing the singer's breath away from the microphone.

Another advantage of the pop filter is you can set it up to be how far away from the microphone you want your singer to sing. Different microphones have different optimum distances away from them—usually four or five inches. You can use the filter to guide where you want your singer to sing, where it's best for that mic.

FIG. 1.9. Pop Filter

MIC PADS

In some cases, a microphone signal might be too hot for your system. *Mic pads* are adaptors that fit in between your microphone and the mic-pre, reducing the signal level.

FIG. 1.10. Mic Pad. Photo courtesy of Shure Incorporated.

For example, I have a really wonderful microphone for recording pianos called the PianoMic made by Earthworks. When I'm recording in my studio, my studio mic-pres can handle microphones just fine. However, if I'm using my portable system, the microphones overload my portable pre's constantly, preventing me from getting a good signal-to-noise ratio. Using a pad helps give me some more headroom.

You might not need a mic pad, but for some setups, it can be helpful.

DIRECT INJECTION BOXES

DI stands for direct injection. They let you plug an instrument, like a bass guitar, into an audio interface. The device changes the signal of a "line-level" instrument, such as an electric bass or a guitar, to the level of a balanced signal, like an electric keyboard.

A good DI box, such as those made by Countryman and Radial, can make a great deal of difference. As with everything, there is a range of options, from cheap to nice. I always recommend trying to go for the nicer direct boxes.

FIG. 1.11. DI Box. Photo courtesy of Radial Engineering.

It's very helpful to have a DI box that comes with a pad, similar to the in-line pad for microphones. Some good DI boxes have a filter on them to roll off low frequencies, like the truck rumble in the 60 Hz area, which aren't in the instrument's range. You actually may not even hear it when you record that one instrument, but there can be a cumulative effect. If you're recording four or five different instruments and each of them has a tiny amount of rumble, it can start to mess with your compressor, or limiters, or falsely trigger an audio device unintentionally. Cut-off filters will eliminate that.

Radial makes a great series of DI boxes. You can buy them in stereo pairs, you can buy them in single mono channel, and you can also buy them in multiple channels. The Avalons or the Millennia are really high-end, super clean direct boxes. But for most applications, a good Radial box will do well for you.

ELECTRICITY CONTROL

Let's talk about the different ways to get power to your equipment. Many homeowners typically buy and plug all their gear into a "power strip." Power strips come in many different configurations. You want one that has surge protection. Surge protected power strips have an internal circuit that pops during a power spike, protecting your precious gear. In other words, it is designed to fail!

Some surge protectors also incorporate battery protection. Their fuse will not only pop during a power spike, but a battery will kick in during a power failure. This is perfect for a computer, allowing it to stay on for several minutes while you save and close it down properly. I personally have my computer hooked up to it, as well as a monitor and a lamp (so I can see what I'm doing in the dark). Depending on the battery rating, you can have additional power anywhere from five to twenty minutes.

Nashville has a particularly dirty electric power grid, which can make sensitive recording gear work unevenly. I also see this problem in other parts of the country.

To minimize the effects of this, one of the unsung heroes of a good studio is having a *balanced power unit*. A balanced power unit looks very much like a power strip you might plug multiple devices into. But it's not a surge protector; it's not actually protecting your equipment. Rather, it regulates the electricity coming out of your wall. This gives you a steady power supply, which stabilizes all of your electronic equipment. This can actually give your studio monitors a better, tighter, bass sound.

In some parts of the country where the power supply is particularly unreliable, they have what are called "brown outs." Let's say, everybody on your street decides to use their washing machine at the same time that you're trying to record a vocal. There's then a dip in the power, which can put a strain on all of your equipment, your computer, your mic pres. A balanced power device regulates that. It works similarly to a battery backup unit, where it stores the energy and releases it at a very even signal, giving you a better sound.

FIG. 1.12. Balanced Power. Photo courtesy of Equitech Corporation.

Power strips let you plug multiple devices into one wall outlet, as long as the circuit can handle the power. Juice Goose makes a rack-mounted power strip with articulating lights so you can see into your rack. I like power strips that have a voltage meter so I can keep an eye out on the power regulation into my house—again, because my house loses power all the time.

In addition, I've invested in a *power conditioner*, which is like a more robust and sophisticated surge protector. They can be pretty expensive, but it can save your equipment, particularly if you live in an area with particularly dirty power. They are more reliable than simple surge protectors. Mine has saved my equipment several times.

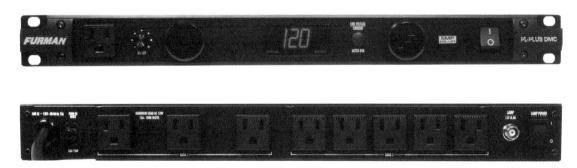

FIG. 1.13. Power Strip. Courtesy of Furman.

FIG. 1.14. Shane's Home Studio Setup. With Robert Neal and Jared Riddoch.

Stunningly good recordings can be achieved in your home studio if you put together the right combination of computer, DAW, and equipment!

CHAPTER 2

The Recording Process

USING YOUR HOME STUDIO

When your gear is set up and ready to go, it's time to record—to use your studio!

There are two common modes songwriters have for using their studio. The first is when you set out to record a song, much like you would in a commercial studio. The song is already written, the guitar parts are worked out, the vocal lines are in place, and the only thing left is putting the recording together. In other words, the studio comes into play at the end of the writing process. The second mode is when you use the studio during, and as part of, the creative writing process. For instance, trying out beats or loops to get the creative juices going (see chapter 6).

Either way, when acting in the role of audio engineer, you want to be able to use your equipment without technical issues intruding into the creative process. In this chapter, we'll discuss how to get your studio ready to go, and look at the overall process of recording in a home studio.

SET UP AND GO!

Let's make sure your essential studio gear is set up, and ready to record.

After making sure the audio interface is correctly plugged into the computer, you'll first connect your microphone and make sure you're getting a proper signal to the interface. You'll then make sure your audio interface is communicating with your computer, and that your computer is "hearing" the microphone and audio interface (so you can record what your mic is hearing). Lastly, you'll make sure you can hear what the computer is processing by sending an audio signal to your headphones and (or) studio speakers.

First, connect your audio interface to your computer. Different interfaces will be connected differently. Some interfaces use USB, some use Firewire, some use "Lightning" connectors, etc. Check the interface's documentation to learn what type of connection you have, and then connect your interface to the proper port on your computer. There is usually some kind of connection LED on the interface indicating a successful connection.

Next, plug one end of the microphone cable into your microphone, and the other end into a mic port on the interface. Usually (hopefully!), the interface is clearly labeled with the word "mic" or "microphone."

Some microphones require "phantom power"—electricity that your interface feeds to the microphone through the mic cable. Instead of printing the actual words "phantom power" on the interface, the phantom power button is usually labeled "+48v," which stands for 48 volts, the amount needed to power a phantom powered mic. Sometimes, there are individual phantom power buttons for each microphone input; sometimes, a single button will engage the phantom power for all the microphone inputs. If you don't see a row of "+48v" buttons, you'll know which type you have! A word of warning: only "condenser" microphones require phantom power. *NEVER* turn phantom power on for a ribbon mic; you'll destroy it! Dynamic mics also do not require phantom power.

Some condenser microphones come with their own power supply box, set between the mic and interface. For this type, you plug the microphone into its power box, and then you use a microphone cable to plug the power box into your interface.

Once your mic is plugged in, your computer can receive an audio signal.

So, open your DAW, create a new project, and then create an audio track in your DAW.

Each audio track will have an "input" choice selector. Choose the input that your microphone is plugged into. Most interfaces use numbers to indicate the different inputs on your interface. If your mic is plugged into "input 1" on your interface, select "input 1" on the DAW track's input selector.

Once your input is selected, you should be able to record.

On the front of your interface, usually next to where your mic is plugged in, look for a "signal indicator" light. It is usually a single green LED light that flashes when you talk into the mic. Some LED lights perform double duty and turn yellow when your signal is almost too strong, and then turn red when the signal is overloading the channel. On other interfaces, instead of a single light, there are a series of green lights (indicating weak to strong signals), yellow lights (indicating a signal is getting close to overloading), and red lights (indicating you've gone too far—too MUCH signal!).

To set a good mic level, play or sing into the mic at whatever the loudest portion of your song is with the input knob set to the lowest level. Turn up the input knob until it starts to *clip*—meaning, the red light on the front panel of your audio interface starts blinking, saying, "Hey, the signal's too loud." Keep singing/playing, and turn the control down a little bit, enough that your loudest note causes the yellow light (or lights) an occasional blip. You are fine as long as you don't engage the red light.

If you're not getting a signal, first check the audio preferences in your DAW, making sure that the right sound input source is active in your device setup. Every DAW program has a place to switch between the computer's internal audio card and your audio interface—usually, a dropdown menu, showing your brand and model of interface. Following that selection, there's always a sub-menu showing how many microphone and instrument inputs and headphone/speaker output channels your audio interface has. Here, there should be a way to select which input and output channels you will utilize for your session.

Once that is set, you should be able to adjust the recording level, which might be on the audio track you created or on a screen associated with that track.

Next, "arm" the audio track for recording. There's always a red Record Enable button on the track, which "arms" the track, allowing it to be recorded on. Whatever tracks have the Record Enable button activated will record.

If it still doesn't record, confirm that there's no "mute" button engaged on the track.

Also, make sure you can hear what you are recording. Every DAW also has a "Track Monitor" button (usually, it's a yellow button right next to the Record Enable). When engaged, the Track Monitor enables you to listen to the live sound of the microphone. When it's disengaged, you will hear the recording of the track during playback, instead of the microphone.

When recording audio, DAWs show a waveform being drawn as a visual indicator of the sound wave being recorded. These waveforms look like blobs. Bigger blobs are louder, smaller blobs are softer.

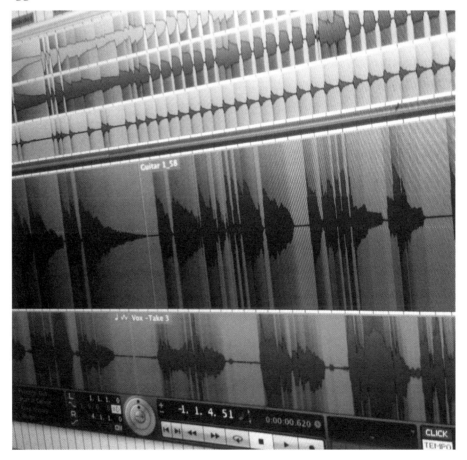

FIG. 2.1. Waveforms

If you hear a loud screeching noise when you arm the track, that is "feed-back." Feedback occurs when your microphone picks up the sound from your audio monitor speakers. To avoid that, use headphones. Turning off that Monitor button also stops feedback.

Then, you can record your song.

When you're ready to record another track, simply create another audio track in the DAW, select the Record Enable for the track, set the signal level, and press "Record." Remember that any track that has the Record Enable button activated will record. Make sure to turn it off for any track you do not want to record over.

If it's only a certain part of the song you want to record over, put the cursor at the beginning of that section, and you can record over just that section. If you want to record for the entire song, place the cursor at the beginning of the song.

If you are using speakers in the same room you are recording, make sure they are muted during recording, so that the microphone does not pick up the sound of the speakers, in addition to the performer. Use your headphones to listen to the tracks being recorded. After recording, unmute your speakers to listen to playback.

CREATING A MIXDOWN

When you're done recording all your tracks, you will then create a "mixdown," the finished version of your song. Different DAWs use different terms for mixdown. You may see it called "Save," "Bounce," "Render," "Audio Mixdown," or "Audio Exporting." Essentially, they mean the same thing: all the tracks are mixed together and combined into a single track.

Most of the time, you're creating a single *stereo master track*, which is a combination of a left and right channel. An audio mixdown will read all of the information stored in each of your channels, meaning: the recorded sound, EQ settings, reverb settings, and MIDI settings. It will put it through the *output bus*, the main output on your DAW, usually at the far right-hand side of the mixer. That final channel's settings will control the final mix.

When you save, you'll be prompted to pick what type of file to create: WAV, AIFF, MP3, and so on. There are an assortment of options for each file type. Do you want a mono file? Do you want a stereo file? Do you want the resolution to be 16-bit? Do you want the resolution to be 24-bit? The lower the resolution, the faster it will render. Higher resolutions take longer, but the sound quality will be better. The higher the resolution, the larger the final file will be. CD quality is 16-bit. I recommend recording at least 24-bit.

TROUBLESHOOTING YOUR AUDIO SETUP

The most common problem in a home studio setup is that the system isn't picking up the microphone. A similar problem is the presence of digital noise. In either case, something is going wrong with the signal.

To troubleshoot the problem, start from the outside and work your way in. Begin with the mic, and trace the path to the DAW.

Is the mic plugged in correctly? I've had that problem. If there's a power supply on the mic, is that power supply turned on? If the mic does not have a power supply, is it a phantom-powered mic, and is the phantom power on your audio interface turned on? If the phantom power is turned on, is the level set correctly? Is your input gain on your audio interface turned up to where you're getting some kind of reading? Again, you turn it up until you get clipping, and then you turn it back a little bit so that there's no clip.

That pretty much addresses the possibilities between the microphone and the audio interface. If it still doesn't record, work your way into the DAW.

The first thing to check at this point is whether your DAW is accessing the audio interface. That's usually controlled in some kind of device menu, and the most common problem is your computer has reverted back to reading its internal mic. So, change that from the internal mic to the audio interface. Most home recording studios only have those two options. (Commercial spaces might have several audio interface choices.)

Once the audio interface is selected as the default input and output, you then check your channel to see if it is accessing the correct input channel. Then the last thing to check is if your output is set to the correct output channels.

Usually, if you follow those steps, you'll solve the issue. If those aren't working, it's usually one of the buttons on the channel. Confirm that Monitor and Record Enable are engaged.

Occasionally, a piece of hardware (mic, cable, etc.) physically breaks, but it's rare. Usually, the problem of not getting any sound is found in the chain described above. Occasionally, with a lot of use, a connection might come loose and might need to be resoldered. But assuming everything is new, everything should work.

But if you've tried all of that and it's still not working, it could be a mechanical issue. After checking all the above, the next thing to fail is usually a cable. Cables don't fail frequently, but they do fail, and I recommend buying high quality cables up front to avoid that.

Next most common: it could be a connection within the mic, usually the connection point where the cord plugs into the mic. So, switch out the cable or the mic, and then see if it works.

STAGES OF RECORDING

The formal process of making recordings is typically broken down into three phases.

1. **Preproduction** is when you get ready for the session: writing the song, preparing your lyric sheets and chord charts, hiring the musicians, communicating what you will be recording, booking the studio, and so on. It includes all the preparatory steps before you actually hit Record.

2. **Production** is the recording process itself: committing performances to a recording medium.

3. **Postproduction** includes editing the tracks and getting them ready for the consumer, including mixing and mastering.

In this chapter, you'll get an overview of these tasks, to help you get started. We'll go deeper into many of them later in the book.

PREPRODUCTION

Beyond the creative songwriting tasks and scheduling tasks you'll need for your session, some preproduction strategies will help you make your sessions go more smoothly, and end with a more satisfactory result.

Designing Your Personal Sonic Landscape

Before you record, it can be helpful to first go through your favorite recordings and articulate what you like about them. You will eventually find some commonalities woven throughout your favorite music. Then, you can deliberately incorporate those universal elements into your own recordings. It's a way to arrive at your own, authentic sound.

Know your "sonic landscape"—your personal preferences for what sounds you have an affinity towards. Do you like a high tinny piano sound, or a dark piano sound? Do you prefer more of an acoustic sound with acoustic guitar rhythms? Or is it a synth sound with more of a hip-hop beat? Or is it EDM (electronic dance music), with lots of pads? Start with your favorite genres, and then dig in to more specifics. Start with, "I like this chorus of this song." Well, what exactly is going on in that chorus? Perhaps they do a stutter edit on the vocal that builds into the chorus, and there is a drop out of all the instruments except for the bass drum to give it space, then the electric guitar solo comes in, highly distorted. So, those are six or seven elements of one chorus. Then, consider which of those elements would work well in your own recording.

That way, you're being true to yourself without necessarily copying somebody.

This process is a gigantic portion of preproduction: knowing what you want to sound like, and knowing specifically what you want to do in what sections of your own songs. It comes down to trying to echo what's going on in your favorite music, without actually copying it.

Which Song to Record

If you are recording several songs, the order you do them in can have an affect on how your sessions go. I like to give myself some instant success, so I do what I call "2 and 1." Two easy songs, and then a hard song. Success early on in the process makes the harder songs easier.

Setting a Schedule

Mapping out a time frame for your project is another important preproduction task. When will you start the recording, and when are you going to be finished with the track? If you don't put some limitations on your project, you could literally record forever and ever, and never get a project done. Setting aside regular time throughout the week, budgeting your time, and making a production list all help to keep your progress moving.

Then, consider the work you need to do. There need to be tracks set up and strategies ready for all the different instruments, whether it's just you and your guitar, or a rhythm section, some loops, and so on. If you've got a band, you might need to produce some sort of charts for those musicians. You might also create some informal scratch tracks, such as guide vocals or samples of types of solos you'd like your players to provide.

Usually, recording the actual vocals takes the most time. Then, there's the editing process, comping tracks together using multiple takes (see chapter 7).

So, you're not only setting aside the time to record the different instruments; you also need to set aside time for the actual editing and mixing. As you do more projects and develop a regular comfortable work flow, you'll get a better sense of how long it actually takes you to finish a song, and then you can budget your time accordingly.

How Much Time It Takes to Record

The amount of time you'll need to record a song will vary. With amateur recordings, you're typically dealing with people who have full-time jobs and other home life and family responsibilities, and you may only get time once a week. The process can take months. Actual time spent in the studio might be a couple weeks, but the process takes a long time. Those projects are harder to stay with.

For more professional projects, it can go faster. You'll typically record the rhythm section first, and then cut all the tracks. With the guys I'm using regularly now, we do a morning session and an afternoon session, and we can get eight songs done. That's one day. Then, guitar overdubs, depending on how many songs, might be a day or two (spending four hours per day—usually, the maximum of productive time a soloist can manage). And then the vocals, depending on the experience of the vocalist, are usually an hour or two per song.

It usually takes a mix engineer a day per song. If there are significant changes to the mix required, that's another day.

A good rule of thumb is that it takes seven working days to record a final, release-worthy single. If you want a live feel, where you first rehearse the song and everyone feels solid on their parts, a song can be produced in one day. Jack White just famously recorded his last album direct to the milling disc on a vinyl mill machine.

All said and done, from first hitting Record to mastering, I would say it takes a month of regular work to record a full album. That's a reasonable time frame, as a rule of thumb, for most artists.

Giving Musicians What They Need

Another part of preproduction is giving the musicians what they need during the session.

Scratch Tracks

It is common to make a scratch recording of a song in order to demonstrate the basic ideas to other musicians. Then you give out the scratch track to the band members, or a singer, so that they can practice to it. After this initial use, it is not intended to be used ever again; no one will hear it.

A similar term, but with quite a different meaning, is "rough recording." The word "rough" is used to mean it isn't mixed or mastered.

Charts

Once the scratch is set, someone will chart the song—either the songwriter, producer, or bandleader. Usually, people make chord charts, rather than actual notation for the song. Lead sheets, which are chord charts with the melody and lyrics, are not particularly common, currently, and seem more of a rarity for home recording. More typically, you'll get a chord chart and a separate lyric chart, or a lyric sheet with the chords written above the lyrics. Whatever it is, someone has to make that for the band. Sometimes, the band members make it for themselves. And some musicians just hear it and can play it without any notation whatsoever. It depends on the complexity of the music.

The players get the scratch recording and the charts, they work up their parts, and then they come into the studio. Ideally, when they show up to your studio, their microphone will be set up, so they won't have to wait. If preproduction went well, the players show up, someone presses Record, and then they go.

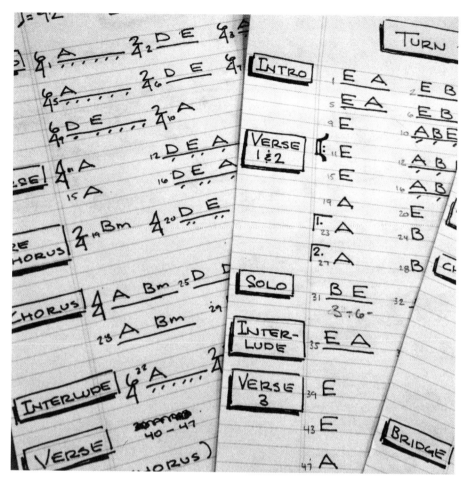

FIG. 2.2. Chord Charts

PRODUCTION

Production is the process of recording performances. There are a few preliminary considerations that can help you save time later on, and achieve a better ultimate result.

Again, there are two approaches to recording a track that are typical in a home studio. One way is to prepare and rehearse everything in advance and then have a recording session. The other is the noodling-around session until you come up with something. Some songwriters like to play around until they come up with a song, and then they'll record their demo on the spot.

There are a hundred possible ways to record a song, and none of them are wrong.

Finding the Right Tempo

Finding the right tempo for a song before you actually record is really important. I like to find a tempo that people can sing the song to. Often, when rehearsing or during the writing process, artists have a tendency to play or sing a little faster on their own songs than what would actually go onto the recording. I'll often have them play it live for me, or listen to a scratch recording, and then back off 7 or 8 bpm when we start the actual recording session. We may try to find the feel by gradually bumping up the tempo one notch at a time until it feels right, and try and find that center. Sometimes, artists get it right the first time. If it's a more groove-oriented song on a guitar—something very rhythm-guitar heavy, those initial tempos are often just right, as they are typically rehearsed. But for other types of songs, I find it handy to back off 7 or 8 bpm, then slowly move the tempo up until you find a nice, slick spot. It's half sorcery: what feels good, what's easy to sing, does it feel slow, how does the timing feel?

I always go by the ease of hearing the lyrics of the song. That's always a primary focus for me as a producer and songwriting educator. I want the lyrics to stand out as much as possible. Sometimes, lyrics aren't as important. In some genres, the lyrics take a backseat. But for most of the projects I personally work on, I'm dealing with carefully constructed lyrics in any genre, so I work backwards from the lyrics.

It's more common for people to rush than to go too slowly. I think there's a psychological element there of not wanting to bore the listener. Speeding up or hurrying feels safe, in performance, perhaps due to a misconception that a speedier tempo creates more excitement for the listener.

I disagree with that. Really, what creates excitement is finding the correct groove, and then sticking to a tempo, whatever that tempo is. Often, slowing something down just a little bit—increments of only 5 or 6 bpm—really pops it into a nice groove. Slowing the tempo usually helps a song more than speeding it up.

Finding the Right Key

What songwriters sing is often limited by what they can play on their instruments, and they don't even consider trying to change the key when they actually go to record a song. But I always look for the best possible key where their voice sounds best.

Luckily, with MIDI and virtual instruments, you can transpose the accompaniment on the fly. You have some ability to transpose on a guitar using a capo, or by tuning the guitar down a step. Sometimes, a step makes a tremendous difference. On a side note, having a home system gives you the luxury to experiment, because you're not spending all this money in a commercial facility where time is money. You can tune your guitar down a whole step, instead of a standard E tuning, see where your voice sits, and whether it works. Or bump it up a couple spots using your capo, because everybody has certain spots in their vocal range that sound better than others.

I use my DAW's Transposition function all the time. I have some really wonderful songwriters, who really can only play piano in the key of C, but they're able to do a tremendous amount because they just record MIDI in their virtual instruments. Then they transpose it to whatever key works best for their voice, singing that specific song.

To find the song's best key for your voice, typically, you'll want to look at the chorus first. The chorus is usually the highest part of the song, and so that's the range where you really want your voice to shine. The thickness of your vocal chords determines your absolute lowest note; everybody has an absolute lowest note. But your highest note is somewhat determined psychologically. Sometimes, people are able to sing a higher note better than a note a couple steps or half-steps down, just because it's in a better part of their register.

The vocal range is divided up into several registers; falsetto is a high register for me, for instance. It's usually harder to sing a note in the breaks between registers, so by moving the song's key/range up or down, you can place the majority of its notes where it is optimal for your vocal range.

A side note: if you understand your vocal range, you can also just write songs in that range, as your default. Then, transpose it later.

TRACKING STRATEGIES

Tracking means to record performances to tracks in the DAW.

Typically, you'll record the accompaniment part first: your guitar part, or your piano part. For a full band, this will be a rhythm section: guitar and/or keyboard, plus bass and drums. After that's recorded, you will "lay down" (i.e., record) your vocals over the accompaniment. Some singer-songwriters prefer to record both guitar and voice at the same time. There are advantages and disadvantages to that.

Let's say I want to record a guitar/vocal, and I'm going to sing as I play. I use one mic for my guitar and another mic for my voice. The guitar is going to bleed into my vocal mix, and my voice is going to bleed into the guitar microphone— that is, the two mics will record both sounds. That's not necessarily a bad thing, but it will limit how much I can adjust each specific sound. That said, there are some really wonderful, beautiful recordings where stuff was recorded simultaneously. Billy Joel and Elton John did that all the time. Elton John built an elaborate device that he lowers over the piano to isolate the piano recording from his vocal mic. So, it can be done. That kind of recording will sound more live; it can have more energy and sound more realistic. But typically, the more instruments you're adding to a recording, the more separation you want to have for that three-pronged mixing process.

After laying down the accompaniment parts, then the vocal part is recorded, then any background vocals, and then any additional instrumentation like a cello, violin, or lead electric guitar part.

The same player might perform the rhythm and lead guitar parts. Typically, the rhythm part consists of strummed chords, either on an electric guitar or an acoustic guitar. Strictly speaking, the rhythm guitarist will only play the chord changes and not add any solo lines. Keyboards can also just play chords like this. I like the term "harmonic part" to refer to whatever is playing the chords.

Typically, the rhythm section records together, to help them gel as a unit. The most important relationship is between the drummer and the bass player. If you have the luxury of recording a band, it's usually the drummer and the bass player you line up. Oftentimes, the rhythm piano part you played will actually get replaced, eventually. It's common to record a scratch harmonic part with the intention that you probably won't keep it. Having the producer or songwriter play guitar with the drums and bass might help them direct the session better. You may use that part as reference material, and sometimes, the only parts you'll keep from a rhythm section tracking session are the bass and drums. Then you rerecord it later, perhaps with a better guitarist.

Rerecording a part over existing tracks is called *overdubbing*. The rhythm section could just be you playing the acoustic guitar, and then you overdub your vocals later.

Full Bands vs. One Player at a Time

Your band might include a group of players performing simultaneously, or it might be just you playing the guitar, then you playing the piano, then you singing. But the process is still similar, whether there's a band or not. The singer-songwriter might only be playing to a lyric sheet because they don't need a chord chart for themselves. But I find having some form of notation in front of them, even if it's just a lyric sheet, is very helpful because they can make notes to themselves, either about what they're playing on their guitar ("I need to be louder here") or a note about how to perform a lyric.

Purely virtual bands are fairly common. Since home studios have become ubiquitous, many professional musicians have their own home studio setups where they can record their parts on their own. You can have all the players play in their own home studios, send their parts to you, and have it sound amazing.

Home studios tend to be optimized for the kind of work we each typically do. A drummer might have a great drum-recording setup, with the right mics always set up to get an excellent sound for his personal rig. As a pianist, I have a gorgeous grand piano in my living room, and some excellent microphones set up for it, ready to record at any time. But I personally don't have the capabilities in my home to record a drum set easily, so my choice is either to send my parts to a drummer to have him record in his own personal studio, or hire out a studio and bring him to the space. It is more cost effective to have the drummer record in his home studio.

Click Tracks

Sending tracks around that other musicians can overdub their parts onto requires a click track—an audio metronome that the other players play to so they know where the beats are. You might record the bass and drums, and then add a click track along with that to help the other instruments (keyboard, vocals, etc.) play along precisely in time.

Putting the click on a separate track lets the other players independently raise or lower the click's volume. For the background vocals, I send a stereo mix of the rhythm tracks (bass drum, guitar), a separate track of the lead vocal, and a separate track of the click, so they can make the lead vocal louder or softer.

Drummers like to listen to the bass, primarily. Typically, a drummer will want to turn down the lead vocal, turn up the bass, and have the acoustic guitar part kind of mid/medium level, and then the click really loud so that they can stay on top. That is a typical way. In chapter 4, we'll discuss click tracks in greater detail.

Producing Other Singer-Songwriters

Having a second set of ears present, such as a producer, is really helpful, both for finding the best tempo and the best range for your song. If you're wearing both hats—artist and producer—you have to get comfortable with truly taking off the artist hat, putting on the producer hat, and listening to yourself subjectively.

Sometimes, your idea of perfection will be simply unobtainable, and you really should just be at peace with going with what you have. Making the call about when something is "as good as it can be" is a vital skill. Oftentimes, instead of having 100 percent, you can get 90 percent, but it sounds really, really great. It will sound great to everyone else in the world. Sometimes, that missing 10 percent is a mysterious area that an artist thinks they can obtain, but they usually can't. It sounds silly, but I'll sometimes tell one of my artists, "Go for the 90 percent."

A misconception is that sonic perfection is what audiences want to hear. Artists often strive to achieve a perfect, pristine sound, where there's no noise, which is actually the opposite of what their listeners want. People want to hear a good performance, and the general public is very forgiving of "flaws" in the recording process. What they really want is a great groove and a great energy in the performance.

Some artists struggle to achieve this in a recording studio. If an artist is a great live performer, I sometimes bring people into the studio to listen to them—like an audience. They have to be quiet! But depending on the personality of the talent and how they react to people, having real live listeners present can make a huge difference in how the artist performs.

On the other hand, you might have an introverted songwriter who is not comfortable in front of people, so you do the opposite of that. Again, going back to that 90 percent of perfection goal, part of that is comparing the energy of performance versus the quirks of your recording environment, of your instrument, the way you sing, etc. Having an energetic performance is preferable to having a sonically quiet performance.

I try to break my artists out of the habit of saying "I don't like that," making the judgment so black and white. I try to put a more positive spin on it. "What is good about this performance? Is this acceptable?"

Just changing that mindset opens up the use of tracks or performances that you might have thrown away because of a little flaw. Also, I'll say that sometimes, what you perceive as a flaw in your performance might actually be a personality trait that your fans, family, and friends actually like in your performance, that makes you sound unique.

A great example of that is Rihanna, who's a wonderful singer. She has this little break in her voice. It's a funky break, but that's what makes her sound like her. I'm sure that there are vocal coaches who would try to get rid of that quirk, when really, it lends character to her voice.

So, we sometimes have to learn to accept our limitations. We compare ourselves to what we hear on the radio, with the thousands of man-hours that go into tuning someone's vocal, that actually might not even be necessary. Instead, sometimes, it is better to accept your performances. Know what your limitations are, and again, ask yourself, "Is this acceptable? Do I like it? Is this a good performance at this time, at this moment, at this space, at this juncture of my life?" If it is, you can move forward.

A recording is like a credit report. When you apply for a loan at a bank, such as to buy a car or get a credit card, they pull your credit report—which is a look at your finances and how you handle your finances at that very moment, on that very day, summed up as a number. Now, your credit score changes over time. Depending on how you handle your finances, it can get better, it can get worse, but on that particular day that is what you have, and those are the numbers that you have to work with. You cannot change it on that day.

The same thing happens in the studio. Are you capable of more? Perhaps, if you practice every day for five hours a day, in a month from now, yes, you might have a better performing ability. But on the day that you're recording, is that the best that you could do on that day? Is it acceptable? Are you realistically going to be able to get an extra riff out, or are you realistically going to be able to hit a note higher?

So, understand your limitations, but don't be ashamed of them. Be accepting of yourself, as you are now. Say, "This is who I am as a person," and let that spill over into who you are as an artist.

Is it an honest performance? Is it authentic? Again, that comes down to who you are as a person. Surrounding yourself with professionals, with a great vocal coach, with a piano teacher, all those things are going to help make you better. And so will listening to your favorite artists and trying to mimic what they do. But, in the moment of recording, try to throw away all of those influences and be present in the moment. Just being who you are in the moment creates the most authentic performance. If you sing a vocal riff because your favorite artist would put a vocal riff there, it might work, but it may not be you.

What are you doing on the fly? What can you have the maturity to throw away, versus keep?

Another aspect of that is trying to be fancy, or showing off. This might work well for someone like Eddie Van Halen, showing off in a guitar solo like "Eruption," or something, has a lot of joy. But trying to show off using someone else's signature technique, or trying to show off doing what someone else has done, is inauthentic. It might work, but it's inauthentic.

Getting Great Performances

Besides being the creative sounding board and guide, a producer is also a psychologist, and a counselor, and a fireman. People can be very insecure in the studio. Hearing yourself in headphones is a very revelatory experience, and sometimes not necessarily in a good way. We do not hear ourselves the way other people hear us, and so slapping on a set of headphones and hearing your voice for the first time can be very disconcerting. And so, I try and create as comfortable of an atmosphere as I can in the studio. I ask my clients what kind of snacks they like. I try to breed a kind of a sense of familiarity in the studio.

One of my clients drinks Coke, but when he records in the studio, he likes a Diet Coke because whatever kind of sweetener is in a Diet Coke is different than what's in regular Coke, and he thinks that makes him sing better. To be honest, I don't think it makes a difference. I think its psychological. But if believing that helps him sing, I'm happy to accommodate him.

Depending on the experience of the person performing, if there's an egregious error, sometimes I will blame myself to help them. My main concern is getting a good take; that's all I care about. So, if I need to say, "Oh, I messed up here in the control room, let's do another one" because confidence is wavering on the other end, I will go there. Some artists like to be joked with, some like complete quiet, some like darkness and candles, some like scented candles. It just really depends. Having a clean studio makes a huge difference.

Communication is very important, letting them know the expectations of what you're trying to accomplish during that session. This is particularly true for artists who are beginning—just starting out.

I'm always more concerned about the performance of my artist than I am about details of what the instruments are playing. As a producer, if you're excited, then the artist will be excited. If you need to be the clown, then be the clown. If it needs to be more subdued, the producer usually sets the tone and the energy of the performance.

Imaginations are very powerful, and I sometimes have artists visualize walking through the performance. If I need you to be more like a model track we've selected—perhaps of a very dynamic live performer—I'll have you close your eyes and imagine you're sitting backstage, hearing the roar of the crowd, and the audience chanting your name. The lights are dark on stage, and they announce your name, a big explosion occurs, and you walk out on stage. Everyone cheers, and you sing those first notes.

Psychologically, that's very powerful and can put them in the moment. I try to take my artists to a moment where they're very successful, through this kind of pre-visualization. Because if you can put them into a mental place where they're successful, you'll get a good take.

Occasionally, I'll have a situation where things are just going wrong and not working, and unless I'm under some strict time constraints, I'll stop a session. One time, my acoustic guitar player switched strings out between recording sessions. He wanted new strings for the session, which is fine, but they were just not working. We were trying things, and I was trying to EQ it to match his previous work, but ultimately, I finally had to say, "You know what? We need to call this. You used a different gauge, went from bronze to something else; we need to get those old strings back. Let's just call it a day." And even though I can be a real cheerleader to my artists, I'm also very frank. I let them know that I want the best performance, and I will stop something if it's really not there. Do you need to practice the part for a day? Let's go back and rehearse it, and then come back and record it.

In production, I try to provide an atmosphere of confidence. I know you can do it, and I'm your friend. I'm your honest friend.

POSTPRODUCTION

Postproduction processes are usually more mechanical and predictable than recording. There are more variables in recording tracks, and more creative decisions to be made. Mixing and mastering tend to have fewer possibilities.

For now, we'll look at an overview of these two processes. Then, we will go into more depth in chapters 8 and 9.

Mixing

When you record, each track's quality is optimized to get the best possible sound for each individual player or singer. But if you play the tracks all together in this raw state, they will detract from each other, and the overall sound won't be ideal.

Mixing is the process of arranging the different instrument tracks in relation to each other, so that together, the recording sounds natural. Essentially, this includes adjusting their timbres, relative loudness, and where they sit in the stereo field.

In mixing, you have three different fields. There's a left and right spectrum in which to put your instruments. There's a vertical spectrum, which is your harmonic spectrum: low, medium, and high frequencies. And then, there's the spatial spectrum: how closely you perceive the instrument.

If you see a band play live, they won't be lined up in a straight line: a vocalist, a guitar player, a bass guitar player, a drummer with all of his drums, all in a row. They're spread out on the stage. Typically, the lead singer is up front, the guitar player is off to the right, the bass player is off to the left, and the drummer is behind everybody. The drummer has his own stereo spectrum of instruments.

So, in mixing, you're basically recreating that band situation electronically. The lead singer is set in the center, the bass drum is going in the center, the guitar player is to the left, and the bass guitar player is to the right. The keyboard part might be spread out for that whole spectrum.

The drummer and the vocalist will be lined up. So, you can tip that vertically. The reason why you can line up a drummer and a vocalist is that they're taking up different spaces of that harmonic spectrum, especially the bass drum, snare drum, and hi-hat.

Sonically, the hi-hat and cymbals are in a higher space than the vocal. The toms and bass drum take up a lower spectrum than the vocal, so they all fit in the same vertical space and horizontal space.

Then, for a spatial perspective, you might put a little more reverb or delay on the drums to make it feel like they are behind the lead singer a little bit. Electronically, you're recreating that stage space. That's what I would call a mid-level instrumentation process.

A lot of singer-songwriters only record guitar or piano with their vocals. The problem is, these instruments take up a lot of the same harmonic space as the voice. If you have a male vocalist playing a guitar, their mid-ranges might be overlapping. To make them fit in a mix, you actually have to choose which instrument takes precedence. So, you might EQ the guitar out of the way of the vocal. If you played back just that guitar part alone, it might sound bottom heavy, but in a mix, it actually sounds nice because you have the vocal taking up that acoustic space.

These are postproduction decisions, after the entire recording has been done, and when you're making spatial decisions of your tracks. You're also making equalization decisions, where parts sit in that vertical space, and making panning decisions, for the horizontal spectrum.

Mastering

Many musicians associate mastering simply with making a mix louder. Mastering can also nuance bad frequencies out of your final, overall mix, as well as improving other dimensions of the sound, and general readiness as a product.

If you have multiple songs, mastering includes getting a general, overall acceptable loudness for all of the songs on a record, so that track 1 is not perceived as having been mixed louder than track 2, which might be perceived as being softer than track 3.

Loudness is a relative figure. You can have a piano/vocal song, versus a hard rock song with a lot of guitars. The piano/vocal might be perceived as being softer than the multiple guitars, bass, drum, Led Zeppelin-fest that you have in your song. But you can increase the perceived loudness of the piano/vocal to match that of the Led Zeppelin-fest song, so that when the Led Zeppelin-fest song comes on after your piano/vocal, the listeners do not perceive a gigantic jump in volume that causes them to adjust the volume of their playback system.

Traditionally, artists took their tracks to a mastering engineer, who worked their magic through various software. Today, there are commercially available plug-ins and programs that help you do basic mastering yourself.

There are creative decisions made during the mastering phase, though, beyond simple loudness levels. Mastering also includes where your song fades out. Let's say that you end your song on an extended guitar solo. How long should that solo last until it fades? And how do you want it to fade? Do you want a linear curve, where it fades out on a perceived equidistant/linear value, versus a curved value? Or should it start loud and suddenly get softer, and then the softness drags out until it's imperceptible?

There are similar considerations for how a song begins. How much space is there between when you press Play, and the actual audio of the song comes in? Is it two seconds?

Mastering also includes imprinting the actual name of the song, the artist of the song, the producer, the genre, ISRC codes, and sometimes other information. This "metadata" can be embedded into the electronic file of that song. All that information is added in at the mastering phase.

Mastering is when the song order on an album is finalized.

Finally, mastering includes the final format with which your song will be heard. Is it going to be CD quality or compressed for iTunes?

Mastering is really the final phase. You can hire someone to do it, or you can do it yourself.

After mastering, the recording is ready for possible replication and then delivery. More about mastering in chapter 9.

THE HOME-STUDIO PRODUCTION MINDSET

Part of being successful and productive in your home studio is simply just relaxing, and accepting the fact that you're recording in your own house, and there are going to be limitations in your home studio versus what you can get from a commercial studio environment. You'll have less control over the sound, both in the studio and from the outside world. You'll have less space to move gear around, fewer options for who stands where, and probably, more interruptions.

You won't be able to get around some of these limitations, so you need to embrace that they are simply differences, and try to see them as strengths. A lot of artists are focusing so hard on getting the perfect snare drum sound that they forget that it's really the performance of the song that is ultimately the most important.

Each room has its own reverb sound, which may or may not be pleasing. You can try to minimize that, but only so much will be possible in a home studio. The great trade-off is that you have much more creative flexibility in your own studio, to record as many tracks at any time of day you like, taking as much time as you need without having to watch the clock. What you lose in technical control, you gain in creative freedom.

Once you accept that the room you've decided to use for your studio will simply be your current sound, it will take a lot of the pressure off trying to turn it into something that it will never really be.

Today's home studio now takes a different role in the creative process than did the recording studios of the past.

The benefit of the home recording studio for the modern songwriter is instantaneous access to your songs—being able to record them that night or that day as soon as you finish them. You don't have to book time in the studio weeks in advance, or hire a whole band. If you just need to record a guitar/vocal, you can do it right away, as soon as you finish the song. So, songs are being demoed much faster, being recorded much more quickly, and getting out on the market much earlier.

Similarly, everyone is able to produce more kinds of products. One of the biggest recent changes is the advent of video media, hosted by services such as YouTube and Snapchat, where people are recording their audio first, and then filming themselves to the recorded audio, which gives you a better quality audio portion of your YouTube video. You're basically lip-syncing to yourself, rather than having to do it live, which gives you the advantage of not needing to wear headphones in your video, and not needing to have all the microphones there. You could film yourself in a very pretty park, and you're doing it just like the big boys, but then you just record the audio in your house, and that makes it so much easier, and quicker. You could produce a video for yourself in a day using your iPhone. Even that small change of using your home recording studio already ups the sound quality of the music in your video. That's a gigantic change.

The ability to collaborate with other people has also changed. There are different software networks you can use where you can connect with a guitar player, or a drummer, or a bass player in another part of the country, where they can actually record onto your DAW. You don't have to have your whole band together in the same room at the same time.

You can also spend more time working on your songs, in a home studio, getting them just how you want them. You can spend some time after work every day, and keep adding as many parts as you want, because you're not limited by time, as you would be in a commercial space. You're only limited by when you think the song is done, which is a great benefit.

So, I'm seeing much bigger arrangements, much fuller sounds. The quality of loops, and the quality of recording equipment, has increased so much that amateur and professional studios alike are now getting much higher quality sounds.

You can iterate when you produce your songs, creating different versions and trying different ideas, to see what works best. You can try a different lyric in the chorus, and then listen to the different versions side by side. And you can get opinions on it, asking your producer, or bandmate, or trusted friend, "Do you like version A? Do you like version B?" You can also try a "vocal up" version, where you mix the vocals at higher levels to see what you like, or what your team thinks works best. You can try different arrangements or other variations rather quickly.

Another huge advantage of the home recording system is that an amateur can do far more professional quality projects than what was previously possible. For instance, if you're into the independent music scene of your community, you can record music to film, and share those with filmmakers. Depending on your arranging chops and your playing chops, there's really no limit to what you can produce.

CHAPTER 3

Recording Live Players

An amazing recording starts at the initial capture of your voice or instrument, making proper mic technique and placement among the most important dimensions of sound engineering that you need to learn. In this chapter, we'll explore some recording techniques particularly for songwriters, who are likely to focus on voice and either guitar or keyboard.

SETTING UP A TRACKING SESSION

Your software is installed, you open a new file, and you're ready to record. Engineers typically talk about two types of recording sessions: *tracking* sessions, where the primary sounds are recorded onto audio tracks, and *overdub* sessions, where small sections within the original tracks are recorded over, either to fix mistakes or to add solos. In this chapter, we'll focus on recording the initial tracks and microphone technique.

Before you start to record, you need to set up the tracks for the session. Each track is associated with one microphone or an instrument that you've plugged in. To begin, a simple songwriter setup will typically have one track (mic) for the voice, and then another track or set of tracks for either a guitar or piano. You might want to add other instruments later, but let's keep it simple, for now.

There are three essential technical considerations during audio recording:

1. **Microphone placement.** This is important for getting the best possible recorded sound.

2. **Level.** You want the mics to capture the sound at the optimum level, and then for the tracks to sound at the right volume in relation to each other.

3. **Panning.** This is where the sounds are located in the stereo field, ranging from left to right and all points in between. While this gets fine-tuned in mixing, mixing is easier if you do a rough panning when you are recording tracks.

Signal Level

At this stage, you want to get as much of the instrument on the track as possible. Later, you can bring each part up or down, so that it blends well with the whole ensemble. To get the best possible sound for a track, you maximize the audio signal at each stage—a process known as "gain staging." Meters within the DAW let you monitor the level of the sound *signal flow*—the path from your microphone to some kind of audio interface, and then audio interface into the computer program. This lets you make sure that the signal doesn't get so loud that it distorts—that the level shown on the meter doesn't get into the yellow or red range.

A typical metering system will have a green, yellow, and red area. Green is safe, meaning there's no distortion. Yellow means you're approaching distortion. Red means the signal is distorting.

When your digital recording distorts, it means that the level is so high, the DAW can't handle that much information. The recorded sound becomes clicks or pops, or truncated sounds. Basically, it will sound awful.

On the other hand, you want the recorded level high enough so that you get the full nuances of the original sound. If the signal is too low when you increase it in the mix, you will also add noise.

To find the ideal level, sing and/or play the loudest portion of your song until you hit the yellow and red meters, and then back off just a smidge.

Let's say that on a scale of one to ten, nine to ten is red, seven to eight is yellow, and everything else is green. Your best results will be if you keep the meter in that seven/eight area. If you record at the low end of the green, at one or two, while you'll be safe from distortion, that recorded part is going to be very, very quiet in the mix. You'll have to raise it up, which also means raising all the noise that's inherent in the room: the birds chirping, the cars rumbling by, even the hum of the computer itself. All those things will be amplified along with the recorded instrument.

You can also use EQ to eliminate many of these sounds, rolling off everything below 60 Hz. While this is generally done during mixing, some microphones and some mic pres have a 60 Hz roll off. This might be called a "high pass" function, meaning they're letting all the high frequencies through. I like to use that function during recording, if my mic or mic pre has that functionality. Again, it can also be done during mixing. There are arguments for both approaches. But particularly for guitar and voice, since their range does not go into the range below 60 Hz, eliminating the range won't make a voice or a guitar sound any thinner. You will only be getting rid of some mud that can creep up.

Instrument Settings for Optimum Recording

The signal starts at the instrument or microphone itself, so the first place to consider the gain level is at the source. Electronic instruments are usually calibrated to perform at their best at certain volume levels. Typically on an electric keyboard, the ideal volume is at around 70 percent, to get the best sound quality.

Seventy percent is a pretty good rule of thumb for most electronic instruments, whether it's an electric guitar, keyboard, bass, or whatever. On some instruments, if you go past 70, to 80 or 90 percent, you introduce noise from the circuitry of whatever instrument you're playing. Seventy percent is usually right below that noise threshold. All instruments will vary (especially guitars), but 70 percent is a good starting point.

The goal is to get the signal as hot as possible before noise occurs, and this precise point will vary from instrument to instrument. Gradually turn it up, and keep testing it, listening to the sound you get. At some point, it will introduce hum from the electronics.

Meters in DAWs inherently allow for some *headroom*: the measurement between the loudest sound you put on the track and the actual moment where it starts to distort. So, even though the meters are in the red, there are internal buffers that prevent the sound from actually distorting. Later on, when you mix, adding EQ and compression will start chipping away at some of that headroom. Some engineers who know that they will use a lot of processing will back down the recorded level to closer to 60 percent, so that they have more room later on for EQing, compression, delay, reverb, or other effects.

A *limiter* adds a barrier to your audio signal so that it will not distort at a setting that you use. You just can't go any louder; you've "limited" the sound. You'll put a limiter on the very last channel on your main outputs, before it goes to the speakers. Set it at about –3 to –4 dB, before your output.

Correcting Phase

When two microphones are set too close together, a flutter might result in the sound. This is a phase issue, resulting from how sound travels. To minimize phase, use the rule of three: the distance between mics should be three times the distance of either mic to the sound source. So, if two mics are each five inches away from the sound source, the two mics should be at least fifteen inches away from each other. This avoids phase problems.

TYPES OF MICROPHONES

Start by choosing the right mic for the job. There are three types of microphones typically used in recording music: dynamic, condenser, and ribbon. They are each well suited to recording different types of sound sources.

There are two main considerations for choosing the right mic: sound pressure level (SPL) and frequency range.

For most uses—guitars, piano, voice, etc.— the go-to studio mics are usually condensers. Condenser mics typically have a large frequency range, meaning the amount of sound, between its highs and lows. A condenser mic will pick up more of that spectrum than will a dynamic mic. If you look inside a condenser mic, it has a "diaphragm," which is roughly the shape and size of a human ear—which is not coincidental. Different diaphragms are made out of different materials, and have different electronics from different manufacturers. Each will capture the audio with varying degrees of color, frequency response, and frequency depth. Condenser mics typically will capture richer sounds than dynamic mics.

Some instruments have very, very high sound pressure levels (SPLs). A kick drum, or a guitar amp turned up to "11" have a much higher SPL than a piccolo. Dynamic mics are really great at recording high SPL instruments.

In the condenser mic realm, there are two categories: solid-state and tube microphones. A sweeping generalization: tube condenser microphones tend to have a warmer sound than solid-state microphones. Ideally, you would match the microphone to whatever instrument you're recording. So, if someone has a super warm voice, you may not want to add additional warmth with a tube mic and might instead choose a solid-state mic. If someone has more of a shrill voice, that might be a perfect opportunity to use a tube mic, which might take some of the edge off.

Most condenser mics require *phantom power*—a 48-volt electric signal that engages its diaphragm. The combination of the diaphragm material and that little electric volt allows the microphone to pick up really intricate, subtle signals.

In my studio, I have two main mics I use for recording almost everything. They both have the exact same diaphragm, but one is a solid-state version and one is a tube mic. Between them, I get an incredibly rich palette of sound.

For a first microphone, most people start with some type of dynamic mic, such as the classic Shure SM-57 or SM-58, which are the most widely used mics. Those actually do a really great job at most things. You do not use phantom power with dynamic mics. So in a bargain basement studio, you can start with a dynamic mic. The typical price for a dynamic mic is between $70 and $120.

A step up would be some kind of studio condenser mic. Most often, the first condenser mic bought is a solid-state, not a tube. Tube mics are a little more fragile, so a really good solid-state condenser mic works really well. They're good catchall mics. Most instruments will sound best when recorded with a condenser mic.

A good condenser mic is going to cost at least $500 to $600. There are some good values out there. The company Avantone has some very inexpensive mics that are typically Chinese made. Many, many mics are made in China, and the quality can vary wildly. The Avantone brand is fairly well built, fairly robust, and they're pretty inexpensive. So, you can get into a good condenser mic for $300 to $400. Audio-Technica has its "40" series. The 4033 is a really good all-around mic for recording vocals and acoustic guitars. Blue also makes some really wonderful mics.

I'm a huge fan of Gefell mics. They are the original Neumann mics, owned by the Neumann family. They have a condenser for about $1,500 that sounds just amazing. Its big brother, the tube version, is about $4,000. I use those two mics on almost everything.

Ribbon mics are really wonderful, and they are experiencing a huge renaissance. In the past, they were kind of hard to use because the ribbon element was very fragile and easy to damage. The mics nowadays seem to be more robust. By nature, the way a ribbon mic captures sound has a much smoother quality than a dynamic or condenser mic. They have a warmer, darker tone. You can use ribbons to record many different instruments. They're really terrific on guitar amps. I personally love using them on upright basses; they sound terrific on them. Recording brass instruments, they sound great because they mellow out the harsher transients. They will also mellow out the harsher transients on a heavy metal guitar part.

Some ribbon mics are also good at high SPL recordings. They tend to have a darker tone than other mics, but can also be very warm, and very realistic. As with all mics, "try before you buy."

Microphone Patterns

The go-to project studio microphone is usually a condenser microphone with a cardioid (roughly heart-shaped) pattern.

Microphone Faces Singer

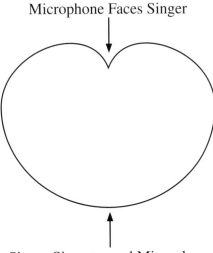

Singer Sings toward Microphone

FIG. 3.1. Cardioid Microphone Pattern

There is an area in front of a microphone that is optimum for picking up the sound of your instrument. *Cardio* refers to a heart-shaped pattern. If you had a bird's eye view of a person standing in front of a mic, a cardioid would have a heart-shaped pattern in front of the mic where the point of the heart is at the mic, and the vocalist would be singing into the globular protrusions. Inside those globular protrusions is where you'll get optimum sound. If you move outside that pattern, you're going to get less of a frequency response, and you'll typically start losing your high and low ends, which can make it sound really nasally. Dynamic mics usually have a much tighter cardioid pattern, which is why they're used live: because they typically don't get feedback or bleed from other instruments.

Remember, inside a condenser mic is its diaphragm, which is like your ear. So, in order to hear something best, you would face your ear to the person. If I moved around to the back of your head, you're not going to hear me as clearly as if I was speaking directly into your ear. The quality diminishes the further right or further left I get from speaking directly into your ear. In a mic, you're substituting the condenser diaphragm for your ear. When setting up a session, I will physically put my ear where I think the microphone should be, and I will physically listen and move my ear around until I find a spot that sounds the best. I will then place my microphone in that same spot, with the microphone's capsule in the same spot as where my ear was. What sounds good for the ear sounds good for the microphone.

On a dynamic mic, the ear is actually straight on.

Ribbon mics have what's called a figure-eight pattern, which is basically two cardioid, heart-shaped patterns. In other words, a ribbon mics picks up on the front and the rear of the capsule, with frequencies on the side being reduced.

Some mics have switchable input patterns beyond the standard cardioid shape. Some have what's called an "Omni" setting, where the mic picks up equally around the entire capsule. "Hyper-cardio" patterns have a very limited area from which you can record into the capsule. Some have figure-8 patterns, like the ribbon mic.

AUDITIONING MICROPHONES

Ideally, in a perfect world, you would first rent a microphone you are considering purchasing. That might not be as easy in some parts of the world. But if you live near a major metropolitan area, there's typically some kind of studio rental place.

I find that on a lot of the blogs, forums, and gear sites, people are incredibly biased towards certain products. Sometimes, it feels rather comforting to read great reviews, but I find that more often than not, those views are skewed—even (or especially) reviews in magazines. Many times, audio journalists will only have the equipment for a day, and they have deadlines, so take magazine reviews with a grain of salt. Let your ears be the judge (or hire someone with "ears" to help you).

A lot of people will audition microphones and only hear them in headphones. You might go to a music store, pop on headphones, and they'll give you several mic options. That's a ridiculous way to audition a recording mic because, in reality, you're not going to be hearing things just through headphones. Headphones are going to add their own color to whatever the mic is doing. That's a worst-case scenario. Best case is being able to get the mic in your own studio, and then listen back to what you've recorded on your own speakers. In fact, listen back on your car speakers, on your stereo speakers, on your iPhone speakers, and on your studio monitors so you can hear what the mic recorded in several different environments. That's optimum.

Understanding the schematics on a mic is also helpful, but those can also be kind of skewed by the manufacturer. Some mics add different color to different frequencies, and that might be a good thing depending on the mic. For instance, the Shure SM-57 and SM-58 actually add a little peak that's pleasant to the ear, which is why those mics have sold a bazillion. But ideally, the best way to audition a mic is to actually record with it and listen to it back.

RECORDING VOCALS

When you record vocals, whether it's you singing or someone else, it is important that the singer's placement relative to the microphone is steady—staying the same distance, on axis with the microphone capsule, and not moving around too much. Some very gifted studio singers can manage microphone levels by moving their head closer and further away, depending on how loudly they're singing. That's definitely a learned technique.

For the newcomer to vocal recording, I usually make a compromise of distance to where the singer won't blow out the microphone. One of the things I suggest, if a lot of passages are blowing out the mic but you're not able to pick up the softer passages of a performance, is to record two different takes and have them move away a couple inches for the louder material. Sometimes it can make all the difference having them sing all the quiet passages closer to the mic, and the louder passages a little further away from the mic.

For beginning singers, I'll put a tape mark on the studio floor so that they know exactly where to stand. Or, I'll ask the singer to stand comfortably and then adjust the microphone to them. (I also do that with other musicians, not just singers.) I try and have them get as comfortable as possible and then adjust the mics.

Some singers tend to "eat the microphone." That is where they are kissing the mic, or singing right up to it. There is some kind of physical contact. Sometimes, it's good; sometimes, it's bad. Usually, that technique is utilized in live performance on dynamic mics where there's a lot of other sounds going on, where, if that microphone was turned up too high, the bleed from other instruments would be picked up by the vocal mic. In that case, eating the mic lets them keep their singing volume down, and avoid too much vocal strain. Ideally, in a studio situation, a singer shouldn't have to do that, but the singer might be used to the technique from their live performance habits.

Using a pop filter as a police line is very helpful to help discourage singers from eating the mic. I actually have a couple singers who sing very softly and have very light voices, and I have to bring them closer in to the mic. The pop filter helps them avoid getting *too* close.

FIG. 3.2. Recording Singer with Pop Filter (Shane Adams)

The enemies of vocals are pops and sibilance, the "s's." Both of those anomalies occur at certain frequencies, and you can sometimes EQ them out. A problem with a pop filter is, in addition to the frequency of the pop (which is usually some kind of low rumble), you're also causing distortion on the actual mic capsule. Even though you can tame the inadvertent frequencies with the pop filter, you still might get distortion on the actual track because of air hitting the actual microphone capsule.

If the singer wears a lot of jewelry, make sure it's not making sounds that will get picked up by the mic.

Isolating Vocals

It is certainly possible to sing and play an instrument at the same time. However, I prefer recording the guitar part first and then singing to that track. That gives you more editing options later, because otherwise, the guitar would bleed into the vocal mic, and vice versa. If you need to change something later, you have limitations if you record everything at the same time. Singer-songwriters who play live a lot typically have an easier time recording each part separately.

Recording vocals separate from other instruments lets the vocalist relax a bit. Otherwise, if one part or the other messes up, you have to do the whole thing over again, and so, sometimes you end up compromising. There's the temptation to keep the whole take without any "mistakes," even if it is a mediocre performance, rather than try to get a new perfect take.

By separating the tracks, you can keep rerecording until you get a really good take, and then you're done. Then you do the next instrument. This allows you to experiment—to try things that you normally wouldn't do, if you were singing and playing at the same time.

Many vocalists will sing the entire song through, and try to get it all at once. Alternatively, you can record a track of only a section at a time and then later on combine the tracks into a complete take; this is known as "comping tracks" together. That's a little more advanced, but it works really well. Another way to comp tracks is to create two vocal tracks; you record the verses on one track, and then record the choruses on the other. That gives you a little more freedom, and sometimes the sections have overlaps vocally where the vocal of a chorus might begin before the vocal of a verse has ended. So, it's nice to have just a separate track of that. This also permits doing manipulations such as making all the choruses a little louder.

Comping tracks takes the pressure off of having to get through the entire song.

The way I personally approach it, is that I typically sing the song entirely through maybe three times. Then I record the verse a couple times, and then record the choruses a couple times, so that I have a total of four or five vocal tracks that I can choose from. Then, I cut and paste the section that I like the most from each of those takes.

RECORDING GUITAR

From a recording perspective, there are two types of guitar: acoustic and electric. You will either plug in the guitar and take the signal directly from the instrument, or will use a microphone, in some capacity. On an electric guitar, you could mic an amplifier. Using an acoustic guitar, you would mic the actual body of the guitar, in front of the strings.

Acoustic Guitar

Most acoustic guitar parts are recorded with microphones. Alternatively, some have plugs on the back that permit *direct input*, with a cord connecting the guitar to the audio interface, without the need for a microphone. An internal amplifying mechanism produces an electronic signal that you can send directly to your recording device, just like an electric guitar.

Having just one guitar track, whether via mic or direct input, can work just fine, and at first, it's probably a good idea to keep things simple. However, many people will record both mic and DI signals at the same time and then use a mix of the two sounds. When I record my guitar, I use two mics and the direct signal. So, I actually have three guitar tracks for a single instrument (panned a little bit, but with my voice in the center). This creates a richer, more natural tone than if I used just one approach.

I point the "main" guitar microphone just a bit forward of the guitar's sound hole, four to six inches away. A good rule of thumb: set the mic the length of your hand away from the guitar (again, roughly four to six inches), and point it at the wood. So, assuming you're facing a right-handed guitarist (with the guitar's headstock pointing to the right), point the mic at about the seven or eight o'clock position of the sound hole. That works well most of the time. If I'm using a second mic, I like to put it over the guitarist's shoulder.

FIG. 3.3. Recording Acoustic Guitarist Michael Hinckley

The main guitar mic gives you the body of the guitar: the wood of the guitar, the strings, the picking sound, and the strumming sounds. The "overhead" mic gives more of a room sound. Then, the direct signal plugged into the audio interface picks up the finger noises, and has a much brighter sound.

In relation to each other, my preference is to have the main mic the loudest, the shoulder mic slightly less, and then the direct signal less than that. I pan the main mic slightly left, the overhead slightly right, and the direct signal farther right. That typically gives a rich, natural guitar sound.

In my home, my living room is a wonderful acoustic recording space, so I can keep a couple mics set up in the corner. When I get ready to record, I can pull them out easily. In a perfect situation, I would have them constantly hooked up to my gear. But I also have a family, which seems to always want to use my studio space as their living room....

Electric Guitar

FIG. 3.4. Recording Electric Guitarist Frank DiBretti

There are two common ways to record electric guitar. First, you can use a microphone set up at your actual guitar amp. This lets you capture your usual sound: your amp, your effects pedals, and so on.

The second way is to record direct, plugging your electric guitar directly into your audio interface. This gives a clean signal. Many audio programs have re-amplification plug-ins that can modify the sound later. You can add amp sound, distortion, chorusing effects, phasing effects, or even make it sound like a Marshall stack. There are also third-party plug-ins that virtually provide all kinds of tones and miking positions.

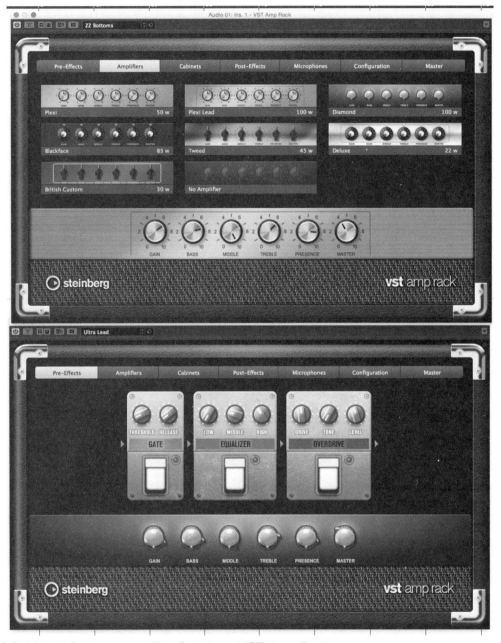

FIG. 3.5. Virtual Guitar Amps: The Steinberg VST Amp Rack

While the simplest way may be to just plug in an electric guitar to one of the inputs of your audio interface, the downside is that this sound might not be as natural as an acoustic instrument or the sound coming out of an amp. Usually, the reason to record this way is a space or a gear limitation. Recording using a microphone at your amp is "better."

You can also use a combination of both approaches: have a microphone on your amplifier on one track and send the direct signal—the clean signal—to a different track, which gives you more options.

Having that clean signal can really provide you with a lot of options. But sometimes, playing only with a clean signal isn't as fun and can mess up a performance. Some people like to hear that distorted sound when they record. So, I recommend that you record the amplifier at the same time as you're recording the clean signal.

Most pedal boards give the option of having a clean signal come out and having the pedals trigger the distortion, delay, or other effect. Some cheaper pedals add unwanted noise or hum, and otherwise degrade the signal, so watch for that. But by and large, you're pretty safe going with most pedals. The guys who know how to use their pedal boards can dial in all their different sounds. Just capture that clean signal as well.

For me, being primarily a piano player, I usually hire a guitar player to play on my own song demo sessions. There are several guitar players that I often use, and I might have specific ideas in mind for them. To them, I can say, "This needs a more Jimi Hendrix sound," or "This needs a more Carl Perkins sound," and they'll dial in those sounds. Guitar players who know how to use effects pedals can find the right sound much quicker than I can. However, when I have time, I find it really fun to see what I can come up with on my own using my DAW's plug-ins.

When I mix, I'll often pan the guitar player's original sound to the left side of the track and then my version, based on the clean signal, panned to the right side, just to give it a more organic feel.

I will also duplicate that clean channel so that I can experiment. One of the magic elements of digital audio editing is that we can copy and paste multiple versions of the same take and try different effects. So, on one track, I might make the sound have more chorus, and on another, I add more reverb, or have one sound more Eddie Van Halen, and so on. Then, I'll choose the one that works best or possibly use elements from several of all the possibilities.

As with vocalists, and all instruments, I will always have the guitar player get as comfortable as possible before I place the mic. I'll hook up the mic before the guitar player gets there. I like the musicians to be very comfortable so that they don't have to adjust to my setup. I adjust to them.

When you're miking musicians, be very conscious of squeaky chairs and squeaky stools. That can be a pain. I like having a little piece of carpet underneath their chair so that if they tap their foot or make other ambient noises, the mic won't pick them up as much. Also, a rug will make it so that their chair doesn't move around.

Also, listen for stray clicks. I just produced a record with a brilliant acoustic guitar player, and his fingernails continuously clicked against the wood of the guitar as he was strumming. I personally like that. It makes it a very natural sound. But you might not want that; you might just want the tone of the guitar. So, be aware of all ambient noises, but especially the ones you probably don't want, such as tapping the foot.

Other things to watch out for, particularly with guitarists: a jacket with buttons on it. When they strum the guitar, the buttons might hit the guitar. Long chains can jangle, or an Italian horn or cross might hit the top of the guitar if they lean forward. To fix that, you can always use a bit of gaffer's tape, and tape the necklace to the guitarist's chest….

Bass Guitar

FIG. 3.6. Recording Bassist Tim Denbo (with Michael Hinckley)

Recording an electric bass guitar is similar to recording a regular guitar. Typically, you are in a "plug in and play" situation, going directly from the instrument through the audio interface (possibly through a DI box, to be discussed in chapter 1). Miking a bass cabinet is always an option, although I know many engineers who record a bass directly into their soundboard. Again, the magic of modern DAWs is you can record a "clean" sound (no distortion) and add grit and distortion later.

RECORDING KEYBOARDS

FIG 3.7. Recording Keyboardist Robert Neal

There are three ways to record keyboards:

1. Recording the audio directly from the electronic keyboard. In other words, connecting the Audio Output port of the keyboard to the Audio Input port of the audio interface.

2. Using the MIDI Output port of a keyboard to record MIDI information, which can then be played back by either a virtual instrument (an instrument opened within your DAW) or synth module. Most contemporary digital audio workstations come standard with built-in virtual instruments. We'll discuss MIDI in chapter 5.

3. Miking an acoustic piano.

While vocal and guitar tracks are typically recorded mono, keyboards are usually recorded as a stereo track, especially if the keyboard is the primary instrument (for instance, a piano/vocal demo, or an electric piano/vocal demo). If the keyboard isn't a primary instrument or a soloing instrument, a mono signal is an option that can make for a better placement in a mix.

Keyboard Audio

Most simply, you can play an electronic keyboard live, routing a cord from the keyboard's left and right OUT port(s) into a pair of IN ports of the audio interface. You then play the track live. This is really the same approach as what we used for the electric guitar going direct—just with a keyboard, this time. A good rule of thumb: turn your keyboard volume level up about 70 percent. Then, adjust the input level on your audio interface to where it falls in that yellow zone. Hitting the yellow is fine, but it should be primarily in the green area. Just don't hit the red zone!

Keyboard with MIDI

The second way is to actually record your part using MIDI (Musical Instrument Digital Interface), and having the DAW play your instrument for you. MIDI works similar to a player piano, where the old paper scrolls had holes in them that controlled the playback mechanism. Instead of paper scrolls, MIDI instruments digitally capture all of the performance information and stores that in a file: the notes, their duration, velocity (loudness), the sustain pedal—everything you're playing. The computer can then associate this information with a virtual instrument sound, and then plays the performance back as audio. For it to work, the MIDI keyboard needs to be connected to the computer, either via USB or with MIDI cables going to a MIDI interface, which then connects to the computer. This is in addition to the audio cables from the keyboard to the audio interface.

The advantage of recording using MIDI is that you can then edit the information, adding or deleting or changing notes and other parameters. You can change the tempo, or fix timing issues if someone comes in late. There are a lot of advantages to recording MIDI.

A very important function of MIDI is *quantization*, which adjusts the precise timing of your attacks, and lets you fix inconsistencies. So, say that you're playing to a click track or drum part, and you're too far behind the beat, the quantization function will line up the beats more closely to the exact beat. Now, this can also take out the human feel of the playing, which may be desirable or not, depending on the style of music. Some DAWs (e.g., Cubase) have a humanization feature, which gives degrees of quantization, rather than just moving everything exactly to a specific part of the beat. This allows little imperfections in the timing, which lets you mimic more realistically how a human player would actually play the part. This way, the performance doesn't sound so stiff.

Eventually, you will need all tracks in your mix to be audio, rather than MIDI, so you will need to capture an audio performance, to translate the MIDI information into a more usable form. This works similarly to how it does when you're playing live. With the MIDI and audio connections set between your keyboard and interfaces, you have the DAW play back that MIDI performance, and record from the keyboard's Audio Out port(s). The only difference is between you playing it live versus the computer playing it using the MIDI information that you recorded earlier.

In addition to the keyboard's native sounds, you can use virtual instruments within your DAW to get additional options for instrument sounds. The same MIDI file can then play back as a piano, an organ, an electronic piano, or even a guitar or saxophone. You record all these virtual instruments more or less the same way, with your MIDI controller. There are several virtual instruments you might come across, such as VST (Virtual Studio Technology), AU (Logic Audio Unit), and AXX (from Pro Tools).

What's really wonderful about using MIDI and virtual instruments is that you can easily try different sounds in your recording. You can record a piano part and then switch the virtual instrument sound to be an electric piano or even a string sound, or you can have a guitar sound playing the piano part. It's really fun to play around with.

Acoustic Piano

FIG. 3.8. Recording a Pianist. (Your humble author Shane Adams, again.)

There is much discussion on how to mic a piano. To me, it depends on whether you're going more for an "intimate sound" versus a "room sound." An intimate sound captures more of the physical elements of the piano: the hammers striking the keys. If that's your goal, set your mic(s) close to the hammers and the dampers. For a more audience perspective, set the mic(s) farther away from the piano, outside its body. I personally prefer the more intimate sound, which is more of the piano player's perspective. My mics are actually set extremely close to the hammers.

I use the Earthworks Piano Bar, which I love. I've divided the keybed into thirds—again, that principle of three. The Bar is three inches up and forward from where my hammers hit. This gives me a really intimate wood sound—the sound of the hammers striking the keys. I love the guts of that sound.

A common and similar configuration is where one mic faces the keys and another is set more towards the bell of the piano's sound bar. If it's a grand piano, open the lid and put one mic towards the center of the piano's bell shape, and another one closer to the hammers, typically a little closer to the treble center. That provides a good mix of those piano sounds, plus you get the warmth, the meat, and the bass of the soundboard. And then from there, you move outwards for a more audience perspective of the piano. If you're miking in stereo, follow that rule of three, if you can.

Most people record a grand piano with its lid open to give it more of an open sound. Others record the piano with its lid closed to create a tighter sound and to prevent its sound from bleeding into the other mics used during the session. Some go further and cover the mic'd piano with blankets and other soundproofing material.

RECORDING DRUMS

FIG. 3.9. Recording Drummer Johnny Rabb

Most project studios don't have the number of mics necessary to individually mic every drum, cymbal, and also the room, as big commercial studios are likely to feature. As an alternative, there's a really terrific mic technique for drum set where you're using four mics: two overheads, one on the snare, and one on the bass. This actually gives a very full and rich sound. You don't have to mic each cymbal. Now, some of the great producers and engineers—for instance, Jeff Lynne from ELO—will actually record all of the drums without the cymbals and then go back and record the cymbals separately, so there's no bleed. But for most applications, overhead mics for all the cymbals work just fine.

One of the most wonderful things about drums is they're infinitely modifiable: different heads and different tunings. A good drummer will adjust them to the sound you are after. I give the drummer a reference, specifying that I want the drums to sound like a specific recording. How do we tune them?

If you are in that mode of recording drums in your project studio, one of the best investments you can make is to have multiple snare drums of different sizes. In a perfect world, we'd have four or five different drum kits at hand, and you'd set each one of them up depending on the project. But you can actually get away with a lot by having the same toms, the same bass drum, and the same cymbals, but switching out the snare drum. There are piccolo snares that have higher pitch, or there are deep snares, and that can make a tremendous difference on your recording.

It's nice to have a little bit of variety so all your tracks on a record don't sound the same. The snare is such a prominent feature of the recording, so just changing the snare can add that variety. If you're miking actual drum kits, invest in multiple snares, when the money comes rolling in, and then probably a good variety of cymbals; different cymbals can also make a huge difference.

Virtual Drums

Virtual drums, triggered by MIDI, are a cheaper, simpler alternative to live drums, particularly useful in home studios. Systems such as Roland V-Drums are really terrific, because they already have different kits set up that you can dial in. I've done several projects just using V-Drums, and the listeners had no idea that they weren't real. Virtual drums are comprised of audio samples of real drums, so they're already properly miked, compressed, and well produced. They sound really wonderful.

Investing in a virtual drum kit might be a better idea, to start, than getting an actual drum kit, because in miking a drum set, you not only have to purchase the drum set, but you also have to get the mics, all the mic stands, and other gear; and then you need a place to record the drums where they don't bleed into the other instruments. Using a virtual drum set like a V-Drums system can eliminate the need for all gear and its setup.

RECORDING OTHER ACOUSTIC INSTRUMENTS

FIG. 3.10. Recording Violinist Susie Brown

Other acoustic instruments such as acoustic bass, violin, mandolin, slide guitar, etc., can use the same recording concepts as the acoustic guitar; for example, placing the mic just forward of the sound holes. As always, let your ear, literally, be your guide. Have your performer play and move your ear around the instrument.

KNOW YOUR ROOM

An often-overlooked aspect of microphone technique is in understanding the room itself.

Before you do a session, you should know where in the room is the best place to record. Definitely experiment. Do test recordings in your room at different locations, particularly for different acoustic instruments, such as guitar and also vocals. Also, try different rooms, if you have options: your office, your bedroom, your basement. Audio will have a different sound characteristic depending on where you are in the room. For example, in my living room—which really has amazing acoustics!—an acoustic guitar sounds very rich, and vocals sound very open and natural and lovely. But there's a spot in front of my fireplace where I get this little interesting bass reflection in the mix. It can either be pleasing or not, depending on the recording. So, I know that this is a characteristic I can use or not use. If it's just a guitar/vocal, it's actually a very pleasing sound, but if I plan a bigger arrangement, that extra bass frequency will ultimately get in the way. So, for those projects, I set the mic at a different position.

Eventually, you'll start using your room not just as a space, but as an instrument. The room becomes another character in your mix.

Too often, people just deaden their rooms. They buy padding, and acoustical tile, and acoustical foam. But I think for the home studio, you can instead embrace the imperfections of wherever you're recording, and it becomes part of the characteristics of your sound. Yes, you may run into some issues, such as barely perceptible echoes in the mix, but I say, embrace those kinds of things, and let that be part of the character.

It's like, does the perfect guitar really exist? Well, probably, and Eric Clapton probably owns it! But each acoustic guitar sounds different. Every brand, every style, every type of string will bring something different to the recording.

I encourage my clients to see their rooms in exactly the same way. Some rooms sound bright, others sound a little more boomy and dark. You can either use acoustical foam and build bass traps, or you can consider how you might take advantage and utilize the characteristics of your acoustic space, rather than completely trying to dampen it—only to add back reverb and all that stuff electronically later?

Have fun, and play in your space. Be willing to experiment and face different directions when recording. Your sound will be unique to your room.

CHAPTER 4

DAW Session Management

Let's talk about setting up a DAW session. You've got the audio tracks, which accept the input. These tracks have to route the signal to an output of some kind (speakers or headphones) so that you can actually hear the recording.

Our goals for the signal's output will change during the recording process. When we record, in order to get the best quality audio, our goal is to capture the sounds at their loudest possible level, before they distort. We initially monitor this to make sure we are getting the richest, most detailed amount of information we can record. The next step is to set the relative volume of the different tracks in relation to each other, and this also changes throughout the process. We do some "rough mixes" during tracking session to help us work with the recording, and we might even have a separate "headphone mix" for every player. Finally, after tracking is done and we have moved to the mixing phase of the project, these relative levels get fine-tuned and optimized for the listener, rather than for the musicians who are still working on it.

So, an audio interface has two types of outputs:

- *Main outputs* go to your speakers, and emulate what the ultimate listener will hear.

- *Headphone outputs* go to headphones, for the engineer and musicians to use during the recording process. You will commonly have multiple different headphone mixes.

For instance, if a recording band includes a guitarist and a vocalist, the guitarist will probably want to hear his guitar louder than the vocals. The vocalist might want to hear the vocals more prominently than the guitar. If there's a rhythm section, usually the bass player wants to hear more of the drummer, the drummer wants to hear more of the bass player, and they both don't really need to hear the vocalist as prominently.

Within the DAW is a mixing matrix where you can send these individual signals to headphone mixes. A separate signal goes to your main outputs, replicating, more or less, what the final listeners will hear.

For a MIDI recording, the input goes to a MIDI instrument (e.g., keyboard) track, and then the virtual instrument track goes out to the main outputs (see chapter 5).

FIG. 4.1. Headphone Matrix

RECORDING TEMPLATES

It's nice to be able to hit Record when the inspiration hits, and not have to muddle around in setting up a session on your DAW. Creating a recording template beforehand, for your DAW, will help you get to work quickly.

Setting up a template is one of the first things I do with my clients, when setting up their home studio system. Then, they can simply open a session template and start recording.

Keep track of the most common parameters you use when recording, and save them in the template session. You will no longer have to recreate all of them from scratch each time you want to record.

I've seen it happen a thousand times: people get so lost in the gear—they get frustrated, they lose their creative spark—because they're setting levels, patching busses, and so on. I try to do all that stuff up front.

Here's how I generally set up the tracks in a basic songwriter's session template.

Click Track	Mono
Countoff	Mono
Keyboard	Stereo
Guitar	Mono
Bass	Mono
Drums*	Mono
Lead Vocals	Mono
Background Vocal	Mono
Strings	Stereo

*(meaning: each drum mic gets its own mono channel)

CLICK TRACKS

Another useful element to use when recording is called a *click* track. A click track is like a metronome: an audible timing reference to play along to. The click sound used can vary from beeps and blips, to a shaker, or various other percussion sounds. Playing with a click can be both invigorating and frustrating, depending on your ability to play in time when you record. Every DAW has an internal click track that you can turn on and off.

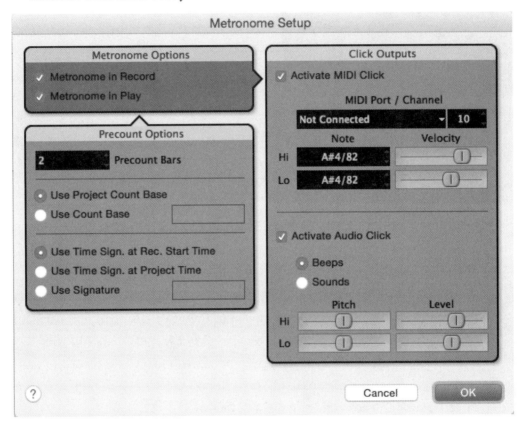

FIG. 4.2. Internal Click Setup

A second option is to create your own click track, create a MIDI click, or use some kind of audio sample. I personally create my own click tracks; I don't use the internal click track on my DAW. I have created several. One has a shaker sound, and one has a clave—it has a more "clicky" sound to it. I have a click that's just a bass drum on the quarter note. So, I have more variety depending on the music I'm recording. Also, since I have different people coming in and recording, I can kind of match what their comfort level is depending on the track.

FIG. 4.3. My Shaker Click Track

It's common to hire instrumentalists to record their parts for your project at their own home studios. For instance, I have a guitar player that I use in Austin, Texas. He's amazing. I will send him my tracks, and he'll record to them. I like to use an audio click track with that, so he can match the tempo of whatever I'm doing, rather than having him pull up the internal click on his DAW, which might be off. Even if it's off by milliseconds, it's gonna be off. But, if he's using my audio click, then that's one less thing I have to worry about.

Countoffs at the beginning help people know when they come in. In a live situation, that's often handled by the drummer—literally, that "one, two, three, go!" In the template I created for my DAW, I have a two-bar countoff that has a really obnoxious clangy sound, which is different than the actual sound for the click track, so everyone knows where the song begins. Some people use a one-measure countoff; I like to use two-measure countoffs.

Rather than starting to record at bar 1, beat 1, it's helpful to include eight measures of silence at the beginning of a session, before the other tracks come in. This lets you align things more easily.

TAKE SHEET

A *take sheet* is especially handy to keep track (no pun intended) of multiple takes of the same instrument. I've seen different engineers mark the various takes with: good, bad, usable, use, don't use, etc.—anything to help them identify what, or what not to use later on in the mix. If your DAW does not have the capability of tracking your multiple takes, a take sheet can save a tremendous amount of time by letting you document what sounds good.

BUSSES

Individual signal routing paths are called *busses*. Any signal can be routed to two or more separate places. The headphone mix and the main mix are considered busses: one signal is bussed to the headphones, and a second signal is bussed to the main outputs.

Now, you might have multiple headphone mixes. Perhaps, I will create Headphone Mix 1, where everybody hears the vocals louder. Then, in Headphone Mix 2, maybe everyone hears the guitar louder. Those two different busses are in addition to the third bus, which is the main mix.

Here's another use for busses. Earlier, when we discussed getting a good guitar sound, we talked about recording both a clean guitar signal and a virtual amp. I might copy that signal and send one signal to a real dirty, grungy amp effect. Let's name that the "Dirty, Grungy Guitar" bus signal. Then I send another signal to a cleaner, more chorus-y, "pretty" guitar sound. That would be a second bus, "Pretty Guitar." You can then audition or mix these two tracks, which were bussed from a single actual performance.

So, a bus is a signal that you have routed. Note that a bus has to connect the track to some type of output; it has to go somewhere for it to be a bus.

HEADPHONE MIXES

The headphone mix is a completely separate mix than the main mix. It occurs on what is called an auxiliary channel or an aux channel, although most DAWs name them as headphone channels, or "cue" channels. So, for instance, say you have a four-piece band: guitar, bass, drums, and vocalist—a very simple setup. In the engineer's mix, all of the instruments might be at a level 8, very even sounding. But the headphone mixes might have several different levels, which you're then sending to the band. On a headphone mix for the drummer, the bass player and the drummer might have a 9 on the drums and the bass, the guitar might be turned down to a 4 or 5, and the vocals down to 3. Whereas, the vocalist might want to hear the guitar, so there's another headphone mix where you've turned the bass and the drums down to 4 or 5, and the guitar to 6, but the vocals at 8.

FIG. 4.4. Headphone Mix

Headphone mixes are very important, but setting up a headphone mix confuses a lot of DAW users. The ultimate goal is to help the performer hear the necessary tracks in such a way that they will give a pleasing performance that you can record. Depending on who you're recording, different performers will want to hear different aspects of the mix. For example, it's very common for the bass player and the drummer to have a very similar mix. The bass player wants to hear the kick drum, and so you will give more kick drum to the bass player. Whereas the vocalist might not care a lick about the bass and drums.

Most vocalists want some kind of reverb in their mix. To help them sing better, or help them feel more comfortable, you might create a "wet mix," where they hear their voice with some kind of reverb.

Another aspect of headphone mixes is managing the click level—the metronome. That's usually a huge priority for the drummer. The drummer will typically want a loud click, but it completely varies depending on the instrumentalists.

You can also set panning in headphone mixes. So for instance, you might put the vocalist dead center at twelve o'clock, and you might put the bass also dead center, and the guitar at one o'clock or two o'clock. And you might spread the drums out over the different toms, and everything across the spectrum to give it more of a natural sound. Some instrumentalists like the click panned to the left or the right. I will often spend extra time trying to get a good headphone mix for my performer because I find that it makes a lot of difference in how they perform.

You can also add compression and other elements to headphone mixes that won't necessarily end up in the final mix. You might boost the vocals a little so that they're more up front.

It's all about the comfort of the instrumentalists or the vocalist who are trying to record. And sometimes, you can actually use one of these mixes at the end of the session. The artist might want to have what's called the "board mix," which is a rough mix of what you recorded that day. A headphone mix can be a guide to what you do for the board mix.

The number of headphone mixes you can provide simultaneously will be constrained by the capabilities of your audio interface. Every headphone mix requires two more out channels. If you need a second headphone mix, that's another two channels. Most audio interfaces have at least four channels to handle that. They'll have one dedicated headphone output, and one left and right pair of monitor outputs. Typically, interfaces are offered in configurations of 2, 4, 8, 16, 32, 64 channels, and so on.

I have my DAW set up to potentially provide three separate headphone mixes, but I rarely use more than two, even though I have that extra channel as an emergency. If you're recording a band, two headphone mixes is very helpful. But if you're typically doing singer/songwriter stuff, or recording just yourself and the piano, or you and the guitar, one headphone channel will be enough.

SUBMIXES

FIG. 4.5. Submixed Tracks

A *submix* is a group mix of several instruments. For instance, I did a record this last year where a really wonderful acoustic guitar player named Michael Hinckley used three channels per acoustic guitar take. We used a main mic (in front of the sound hole of his guitar), an overhead mic over his shoulder to capture a little bit of the room sound, and then a direct signal. So, there were three channels for one player.

Then, we did a group mix. Instead of adjusting all of those signals like a headphone mix, I set their relative levels. The main mic was a little louder than the overhead mic, which was a little louder than the direct signal. I panned the main mic to the center, the overhead mic a little to the left, and the direct sound a little to the right. So, there was a little bit of a stereo spread to make it sound nice for the performer. I then sent those three signals to their own submix, controlled by just one fader on my DAW's mix console. That way, I only had to use one fader to raise or lower the volume of those three mics rather than having to adjust them individually. Once I got the sound really good in the submix, it was just a matter of raising or lowering that one fader for the guitar generally in the mix.

Another advantage of using a submix is that I only had to apply one reverb or one delay to all three tracks, instead of three separate reverb sends. I just apply the effect to the submix.

Submixes are also helpful for drums. Whether you're using a live or virtual drummer, I try to give each drum its own channel on the mixing console. So, the bass drum has one channel, the snare has one channel, the overheads have one channel. Then, I'll do a rough pan and level configuration, but instead of sending them to the main output mix, I will send them to a submix. That way, I only have to use one fader to raise or lower the volume of the drum set, and I can add one reverb to it instead of six, or seven, or eight separate reverbs.

I can still add effects to the individual channels. I might add compression to the snare drum, or I might EQ the bass drum. But the overall level can be changed using that one fader from the submix.

I create submixes for groups of similar instruments. I recently recorded a violin quintet. Even though, on the console, each player had a dedicated channel, I routed them to a submix before the main mix so one fader could turn them all up and down. On other recordings, I have had submixes for groups of mandolins, or submixes for all the guitar mics, or for all pads. By using submixes, there are fewer controls for all the instruments, so I can make changes more easily.

TRACK DOCUMENTATION

Channels/tracks used to be labeled by taking strips of white tape and putting them in front of a console. There wasn't much room for these labels, on old consoles, and so a shorthand became common for instrument names. Guitar became "Gtr," bass became "B" or "Bs," Piano was "Pno," vocals became "Vox," and so on. Many engineers still use those abbreviations.

FIG. 4.6. Console with Tape for Tracks. Photo by Reid Shippen.

Personally, I prefer spelling out the names. And I will name things "Violin 1, 2, and 3." For voice, I use "Vox 1, 2, and 3." For acoustic guitars, I typically will do "A Guitar," and for electric guitar, "E Guitar." But I know that actually annoys some of my mix engineers, so I try to accommodate their shorthand: usually three or four letters, often in all caps. Here are some of the common abbreviations they use.

VOX	Voice
BGV	Background Vocals
B or Bs	Bass
GTR	Guitar
DR	Drums
PNO	Piano
E	Electric
A	Acoustic
HH	Hi-Hat
BD	Bass Drum
SD	Snare Drum
L	Left
R	Right
OH	Overheads
DIR	Direct or Direct Box

FIG. 4.7. Engineer Shorthand for Track Names

Most DAWs, in their track listings, have a field where you can write notes. I find it handy to use this space to document the mic, the amp setting, and any other pertinent information, such as special modifications (blanket in kick drum, etc.).

KEYBOARD SHORTCUTS

Another wonderful way to customize your recording experience is to use keyboard shortcuts. Many shortcuts are common across all DAWs, like pressing the spacebar to start and stop playback. Most DAWs have their own set of shortcut keys. You can even buy custom computer keyboards for your respective DAW, with the most common shortcuts preprinted on the keys as a reference.

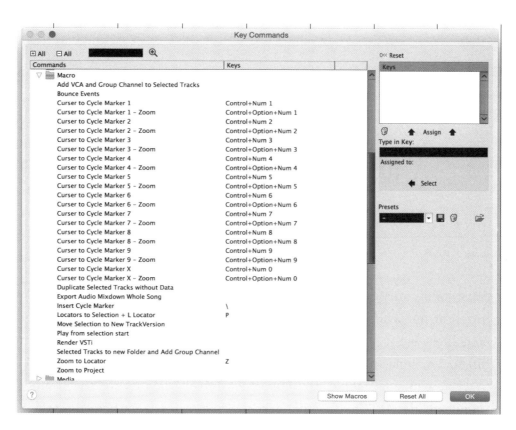

FIG. 4.8. Keyboard Shortcuts

A shortcut key can be assigned to most DAW menu functions. I keep track of my most used tasks, and assign keys to them. For example, a common keyboard shortcut is to use Command-A (Control-A on PCs) to "select all"—to highlight everything within a project. I created a shortcut key where I press Shift-A to select a single track. I then assigned "Mute" to the letter M key. I can zoom in or out using the Up and Down Arrow keys. I've even assigned shortcut keys to open and close different windows pertaining to my project. For example, one key opens my loop browser within my project, and another key opens my media pool (a media pool is where all the audio files pertaining to my project are stored).

You can also automate combinations of tasks—i.e., create a "macro"—and assign that macro a shortcut key.

Keep track of your most used tasks, and assign them to keyboard shortcuts. Keyboard shortcuts will help you work quickly and efficiently.

CHAPTER 5

MIDI and Virtual Instruments

MIDI stands for Musical Instrument Digital Interface. It is a protocol that allows different musical instruments and devices—synthesizers, sound modules, computers, etc.—to connect. MIDI was created as a method for keyboards from different manufacturers to communicate with and "play" each other. It developed to where computers could also interact with the keyboards and their outboard sound modules. MIDI and computer technology advanced to where those physical sound modules and keyboards were augmented by "virtual instruments," which are stored inside a computer and accessed from within a DAW. (Now, many virtual instruments can be "stand alone," meaning: they can be opened and played live without the need of a DAW.) MIDI is the language with which your computer talks to these virtual instruments, outboard synthesizers, or sound modules.

MIDI devices send performance information to each other. The type of information in a MIDI communication includes information about the note. So, if you press a C note on a keyboard, it directs the virtual instrument or the sound module to play that note C. If you hold a chord down, the sound source will perform the chord. Also, if you play the chord loud, it's going to record it as being loud, or it might control the level of sustain. In other words, MIDI communicates all of the performance information. The performance information can be saved in a "MIDI file," which can then be replicated over and over again. So, if you play a scale on your keyboard, your computer can record the performance information for how you played those notes. Upon playback, your computer will play that scale over and over and over again, exactly as you performed it yourself.

You can then adjust those notes in that captured MIDI file. You can change the pitch, the length of those notes, or any other aspects of that performance. So, you can edit and perfect a MIDI performance in ways that are not possible with a regular instrument.

Once you have that perfect performance—once it sounds great—you then patch your MIDI instrument's output (whether internal or virtual) into an empty audio channel of your DAW, and then record an audio capture of that MIDI performance. That captured audio track then becomes editable with audio manipulation tools, such as reverb or EQ, just like any other track.

MIDI information is only performance information. It is not sound information; it is not a particular instrument. I can take that MIDI recording of a scale, and then change the sound in the virtual instrument. It could be performed on a piano sound, a guitar, a xylophone, a kazoo—it doesn't matter. And, I can audition different sounds. I can also copy and paste that MIDI information into another channel, and have two separate instruments playing that same scale. Again, MIDI is only the performance data.

MIDI LOOPS

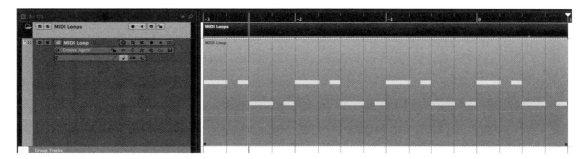

FIG. 5.1. MIDI Loops

Besides just recording your own part with a MIDI instrument, you can buy (or otherwise procure) MIDI loops and use those in your own tracks.

This process is particularly common with drum loops. A great studio drummer records a MIDI track using a MIDI drum set, and then you can plug this track into your own DAW. You can then use your own drum sounds with his drum performance. Your computer reads how he played the different drums, and then matches it with your own own virtual instruments.

While this started with drums, eventually, musicians started doing this with other instruments: piano, strings, horns, guitar solo licks, guitar strumming, and more. You can plug any of those performances into your DAW and then choose the sounds that you want for them. You could also change the instrument. You might take a loop that was originally a piano performance and use your own guitar sound to play the notes, or a horn section. So again, the performance and the actual sound are two separate entities.

REAL-TIME VS. STEP-TIME RECORDING

There are two basic ways to create a MIDI performance: real time and step time.

Real-time recording is like performing any other instrument. You push Record and play, say, a MIDI keyboard, which is recorded into the computer. The computer will record that performance exactly. Once you press Stop, you can go back and manipulate those notes. If you flubbed a note or you played an extra note that you didn't want, you can delete that note, or move it to where the attack of that note occurred. So, let's say you're off with your timing. You play a chord at the beginning of your verse, but you came in late. You can move those MIDI notes right to the downbeats. If you played a wrong note of a chord, you can adjust that one note to correct any sloppy playing.

Step-time recording is where you program in the notes "out of time." You hold down the chord on your keyboard, and then click a quarter-note icon, and the computer enters that chord as a quarter note. Or, you can use a mouse to enter the notes. Then you go to the next beat and click in another chord, and then you go to the next, and on and on throughout the entire piece. This way, you're actually not playing to a metronome, and you're not playing to a beat. You're going step by step through your entire piece. You can also program in the note's "velocity" (i.e., how loudly you will play it). So, you might choose a soft half note, and then the next note might be a very loud quarter note, and then the next note, a mezzo forte chord, and so you just step your way through the entire performance. It plays back in perfect time, so you have the perfect performance.

Many people use a combination of both approaches. On a real-time recording, it's common to record at a much slower tempo that you can actually play at. Then, you speed up the tempo, and the MIDI notes will follow whatever tempo you choose. Let's say you write a blazing killer solo lick that you can't play for your life. Instead, you can either punch in the notes individually in steps, or you can perform and record it at a very, very slow tempo, and then play it back up to speed.

You can also cut and paste sections and modify them to suit new keys, tempos, or other variations. Let's say you record a piano part that you really like on a verse, but for the life of you, you cannot duplicate it for your second verse, which is in a different key. You can simply copy and paste it, as you could with an audio performance, but also, transpose it to the new key. It's exactly the same performance, just modified to suit the new location. You might do that with a lick, or with a chord pattern. And, of course, you can do just regular repetition. If you've got a repeated piano chord pattern of four or five chords, you then copy and paste it throughout the entire song. You don't have to play four minutes of the same chord progression. Just paste and paste and paste and paste and paste, until you've reached the four-minute mark of your song. Or, some DAWs will let you simply indicate how many times it should repeat. It's a very useful and very handy technique.

BUYING MIDI FILES

One useful approach is to buy MIDI files for a commercially released song. Many musicians and companies create complete MIDI sessions for famous songs. Let's say you like the drum part and the synth part of a U2 song, but don't need any of the other instrumentation. You can buy the song, and then copy and paste just those parts that you want to use in your own song. Then, you can go in and adjust them to suit your own work. You can change the notes or key, you can change it from a major key to a minor key. Because it is MIDI, you can easily manipulate any of that information. This is a way to get yourself up and running very quickly in a style that you like, when maybe, you don't have the time to work through and create all of those parts yourself.

You can also use different elements from different songs. Let's say you have a rock beat from a heavy metal song. You cut and paste the drum part into your DAW session. Then, there's a really cool guitar lick or guitar riff from an R&B song. You can cut and paste that and put it into your song, too. So, you can mix and match different elements to create a unique performance.

Third party songs typically have the instrument information embedded into the download. If I buy a Katy Perry song, it may come with fifteen or sixteen tracks. Track 1 will be the bass, track 2 will be the piano, track 3 will be the rhythm guitar, track 4 will be the lead guitar, track 5 will be the drums, and so on. You have the choice of importing into your session all fifteen of those tracks, or you could import just the piano part, or import just the drum part, etc. Again, then you can go in and manipulate any way you want: pitch, length, velocity, or whatever.

VIRTUAL INSTRUMENT SETUP

FIG. 5.2. Virtual Instrument Rack

A virtual instrument might be set up in a couple different ways, depending on the type of DAW you use. For the more modern systems, the DAW will create an "instrument track," which is a hybrid of a MIDI and an audio track. In traditional audio recording, if you're recording a saxophone, you would record it on an audio track. A pure MIDI track is just performance information. The older technique was to record your performance on the MIDI track, and then route that MIDI performance either to an external MIDI device, sound card, or a virtual instrument, so that it could then drive audio information.

Relatively recently, the DAWs combined the MIDI track and that virtual instrument track to where the virtual instrument will read your MIDI information. You still record MIDI information, but it is automatically output as audio. So, instead of having two tracks to deal with, you will only have one. You see the changes instantaneously, and your computer sees it as one track. It appears as one track on your interface. It retains the MIDI information, and then you also have the choice of which virtual instrument you're going to use to play back that MIDI information. In other words, you can change from the saxophone to the guitar, or whatever, more seamlessly and intuitively.

On older systems, instead of having a dedicated instrument track—which again combines the virtual instrument and the MIDI information—you need to create and set up a separate MIDI track and virtual instrument track that the MIDI track is routed to.

On your display, when you're recording, you'll see the MIDI information, which looks like little blocks. On your virtual instrument track, you'll see the regular audio WAV file.

MIDI HARDWARE

To record MIDI information, you have to have some type of MIDI controller. The most typical one is some kind of keyboard controller. These come in all shapes and sizes: 88 keys, 76, 31, and they even have little mini ones, with just two octaves.

Besides keyboards, there are wind instruments that have the keys of a saxophone.

There are also drum machine modules, which have all kinds of different pads and configurations, where, instead of having typical piano keys, you'll see a row of squares. In square 1, you can insert your bass drum, square 2 the snare drum, square 3 the tom tom, etc. Literally, they're "beat boxes," which is where we get that term.

In more modern DAWs, as I mentioned, you can record your voice into an audio track, and then have your DAW analyze that vocal recording and export a MIDI file based on what you sang.

Let's say you want to create a little sax solo, but when you play it on a MIDI keyboard using your fingers, you stumble and fall; it sounds like a keyboard, rather than a wind instrument. You could fix the performance via MIDI, to make it sound more like a wind instrument, or you could instead sing the pattern, convert it to MIDI, and have that MIDI channel play your sax part. This way, you are likely to end up with a performance that sounds much more like an actual saxophone.

A lot of people are scared of MIDI because it involves digital information, which tends to make a performance sound more robotic, rather than fluid, with the sound of real instruments. Think of MIDI as performance information that you can adjust to create a performance that sounds like a human performed it and not a computer. So, you get a good performance, and then you match that performance with a piano part, a drum part, guitar part, or whatever you need. You can easily switch the instrument sound in the part. This means that if you get the performance right, MIDI can make different instruments more accessible for your recording, compared to hiring live players for every part. But the performance has to make sense for the instrument sound you want to use.

Another reason why MIDI sometimes has a reputation of having inferior quality is the over-reliance of General MIDI (GM). General MIDI is a list of very common instruments. When you load your performance into your DAW, your DAW asks you if you want to use the GM information. Typically, it will automatically load the GM instruments. GM instruments are usually a lesser quality than other virtual instruments, but they're good for getting a good idea of how something sounds. Then, you can tweak it with your custom instruments.

Another type of gear you'll see is a MIDI interface, which is typically used when you're using outboard MIDI instruments or hardware sound modules. If you're using only virtual instruments that are contained inside the computer, you don't necessarily need a MIDI interface. Most MIDI controllers are now USB, so you can plug them directly into your computer, and control your MIDI information using your USB port. But many producers still use "outboard gear"—hardware sound modules. In order to control them, you'll need a MIDI interface, which acts as a router. You then play your keyboard, and instead of using sounds internally from that keyboard or computer, it triggers the notes and the sounds from your Roland, or Korg, or Yamaha devices—there are a thousand different companies. MIDI interfaces are not as prevalent as they used to be, but they're still out there.

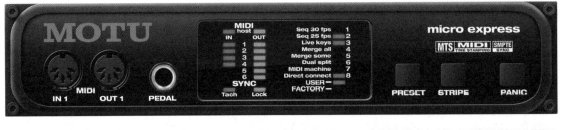

FIG. 5.3. MIDI Interface: The MOTU Micro Express. Photo courtesy of MOTU, Inc.

A MIDI "Y" cable lets you plug some older keyboards into a USB port. One end has a USB connector, and the other has both a MIDI OUT and MIDI IN plug, which you can plug into an older, non-USB-compliant keyboard.

SYNTHESIZERS AND SAMPLERS

Virtual instruments and outboard gear are both based on two audio creation technologies: synthesis and sampling. Most simply, a *synthesizer* uses electronics (or digital representations of those electronics) to produce sounds—either a mimic of a real instrument or something entirely electronic. A *sample-based instrument* uses recordings of actual instruments for playback.

FIG. 5.4. Synth/Sampler

One of the big differences between the two is the amount of memory that they take up. A sampled instrument, which uses actual recordings, requires a lot more memory than a synthesized instrument.

There used to be more limitations of sampler-based instruments due to these memory requirements, but with the advent of virtual instruments, which are placed inside the computer, some of these limitations are going away.

For instance, consider that when you play one guitar string, it makes a different sound depending on how hard you pluck it, or if you strum it with your finger, or if you strum it with a pick, if you strum it hard, or if you strum it softly. Each one of those would require a different sample to play back. Most dedicated hardware samplers only use three samples. For instance, on that pick guitar sound, you'll have a low, medium, and high volume. But on a virtual instrument, you might have ten or fifteen levels of velocity, so virtual instruments sound incredibly nuanced and incredibly realistic.

Imagine a piano, which has eighty-eight notes. With the old sampler technology, you basically have three levels of all eighty-eight notes. There were also limitations on the number of notes that could sound at the same time. Some instruments were limited to eight notes or sixteen notes. With virtual technology, you can play all eighty-eight notes (which you normally wouldn't do!) at twelve or fifteen levels of velocity, each one of those velocities having a different sound. You can also add the sound of the hammer noise against the string. There's literally a little physical click that you can add, too. You can add the damper pedal or the sustain pedal; there's a noise on a real piano that occurs when you push a pedal down that can be added. You can add a soundboard resonance to the guitar or the piano. There are all these extra elements that take up tremendous amounts of memory that you can utilize in a virtual instrument on a computer, versus a hardware instrument.

I was originally frightened by MIDI, but now I embrace its ease of editing and its ability to give me performance options I might not have considered. I view the purchase and use of MIDI files as if I was hiring a musician to personally come to my studio and play the parts. For songwriters, MIDI is the hidden gem.

CHAPTER 6

Using Loops in the Creative Songwriting Process

A "loop" is a snippet of audio or MIDI that is designed to be repeated. It could be one, two, or eight measures long, or even the duration of a whole song section.

DAWs come stocked with their own loops. You can also purchase individual loops and entire libraries of loops online.

There are two loop types: audio and MIDI. As we saw in chapter 5, MIDI allows you to access instruments and their sounds. MIDI loops go a step further by allowing you to access performances of the instrument, such as a rhythm guitar or drum part.

Loops enable you to explore musical territory that you might not have considered otherwise. Many songwriters now start the songwriting process with a loop. A cliché is that songwriters tend to write just ballads—slow-tempo songs. To avoid that, we can start with, say, an up-tempo rock drum loop, with a rock bass line. This forces us to explore a musical direction different than where our usual habits might lead.

The wonderful thing about loops is that you can create complete arrangements for your songs without having to hire professional musicians. Loops can be $20 to a couple hundred bucks. This might seem a little steep for a loop, but if you're paying a musician $1,500 a day, it can be a great cost savings.

There's no limitation to how you might use loops. You can take an R&B vocal background loop on a heavy-metal drum part, with a jazz acoustic bass line, and mix and match to make your own.

Loops are a true blessing for the smart songwriter trying to record their songs. Few of us are multi-instrumentalist geniuses. Instrumental loops allow us to feature amazing musicians in our recordings, and they can play in every genre and style. Need a funky clavichord for a dance tune? Bam! There are loops for that! Need a spacious reverb-y rhythm guitar backdrop? Bam! There are loops for that! Metal riffs? Done! Ska horn parts? No problem! Whiny pedal steel for your country song? You're in!

The best place to start accumulating your own personal instrumental loop library is to do an honest assessment of yourself, and buy for your weakness.

These questions are a good place to begin:

- What genre of music am I writing?
- What instruments would I hire, if I could?
- What can I already play?

One of the best aspects of using loops is that they allow you to experiment during the writing process. I find a great sound and/or a great groove can really get the creative juices flowing. For example, my main instrument is piano. I can usually play 90 percent of what I need, myself. I'm an adequate guitar player, with strengths in fingerpicking, but I struggle with my rhythm guitar playing, so that is where I started assembling my own loop library. I'm also not a great rock/Jimmy Page lead player. But I can buy loops with Jimmy Page-sounding licks, and then I can write a Led Zeppelin-esque song, and have it turn out pretty close—at least, in terms of sonic quality. I started buying up electric and acoustic guitar rhythm libraries to augment what I couldn't play.

As a result of incorporating the use of loops into my work, I became a new writer and expanded my songwriting chops into new genres. I could go for a gritty grunge sound, or a screaming hard rock, chunky metal, or clean pop rhythm guitar sound. I was now no longer limited by my piano skills.

Many loop libraries are available that include several instruments. For example, you can purchase a blues guitar library and its companion blues bass library, to round out your rhythm section.

Electronic music—dance, dubstep, rave, ambient, etc.—is especially well served by loop libraries. There are hundreds of cool synth loops and pads to facilitate your next dance hit.

Another set of instrument loops I use are brass and string libraries. I love adding horns to punch up a song. Brass libraries come with solo lines and licks, sections of single instruments (like a four-part tenor sax section, or five trumpets), or multiple-instrument sections (sax, trumpet, trombone, etc.). There are stabs, licks, hits, guide tone lines, etc., all providing different types of color for your composition.

There are similar libraries for orchestra and strings. A string library typically consists of, well, strings: violins, violas, cellos, and double basses (i.e., upright basses). An orchestra library will have all the instrument families: string sections, woodwinds (flute, oboe), brass (French horns, etc.), and orchestra percussion (timpani, tubular bells, etc.). There are some terrific string and orchestra libraries geared towards movie soundtrack creation, in addition to background parts for songs.

Like brass libraries, string/orchestra libraries provide a generous helping of ideas. You can find solo violin lines, weepy cello passages, thunderous orchestra stabs, etc.

I also use loops of vocal phrases for background "oohs" and "ahhs" and "doo-wops" and "doots."

MIDI LOOPS

As we discussed in chapter 5, virtual instruments have become so good that it is often hard to differentiate a real acoustic instrument from a virtual instrument played using MIDI.

There are lots of loop libraries for MIDI parts. Primarily, you'll find a wealth of drum and percussion loops. MIDI performances for other instruments, such as piano, horns, strings, and guitars, are also available as loops.

A cool trick for working with MIDI loops is to purchase a complete MIDI arrangement of a favorite song that you're trying to sound like. There are programmers out there who like to create perfect MIDI reproductions of thousands of songs in every genre. In other words, with the right virtual instruments, the MIDI arrangement could sound just like the record (minus any vocals, of course). You can have five to sixteen or more MIDI tracks of all (or most of) the instruments on the original record.

Here's where my trick comes in. I'll buy the MIDI arrangement of a song that is close to what I want my song to sound like, and I'll extract only one or two parts, like a great bass line, keyboard, or guitar part. Yes, you have to watch out for "signature" licks (which are under copyright), but oftentimes, the non-signature parts are highly usable, and you can extract individual parts for your project. Not only that, but because you have your own virtual instruments, you can use a completely different sound (or instrument) for the MIDI part so that the output barely resembles the original.

You can also mix and match MIDI parts from completely different songs to create your own custom sound. For example, take a bass from a 1980s rock song, put it with a percussion loop from a 2005 hip-hop hit, layer a keyboard from a '90s pop song, and a guitar part from a '90s grunge tune. There are no limitations.

A good way to practice is to take three or four MIDI versions of songs that are similar (for example, three or four songs from '60s Motown) and construct an arrangement using a different instrument from each of the songs to create a "new" song.

You can even mix up sections. Take the piano from the verse of one song, the horn section from the bridge of another song, and the guitar groove from the chorus of another. Your listeners aren't going to know where you got the parts. Of course, you'll have to make sure it's all set up with the same key and similar chord changes, but you can really get a tremendous amount of mileage by mixing and matching MIDI files from different songs.

Remember, a MIDI loop contains the performance of the part, but not the sounds. You choose your own virtual instrument to play back the performance. The quality of your virtual instrument will determine the quality of the sound of the performance.

MIDI files come in two different varieties: a Type 1 and a Type 0 file. In a Type 1 file, individual parts are saved on different tracks. In a Type 0 file, everything is merged into a single track. (There used to be a Type 2 file, but it never caught on.)

AUDIO DRUM LOOPS

Audio loops from recordings of acoustic drums are particularly useful in creating drum parts. Many singer-songwriters play guitar or piano, but songwriter drummers are less common, so drumbeats are a particularly common candidate for looping. You can just purchase a drum loop, set it in your software, and have your own virtual drummer playing the part for you.

FIG. 6.1. Drum Loop

A lot of loops come packaged as a set of verse, chorus, bridge, and intro loops, so you can insert them into your song and create a drum arrangement. This is very handy. Now, you're not limited by style or by what you can perform personally. If you wanted to do a Brazilian tune, you could buy Brazilian beats played by experts at that kind of music, on appropriate instruments. There are heavy metal drum loops; there are non-genre specific loops. You are only limited by what you can find.

Relying on loops started in hip-hop, often used by samplers, which are dedicated devices that are optimized for the purpose. Sampler capabilities later became incorporated into DAWs, and most of them have the ability to incorporate loops into arrangements.

Looping started with drums, but then other instruments started getting into the "loop game." Rhythm guitar parts are another useful type of loop. You can find them for different guitars: Telecaster, Stratocaster, and others. Do you need a funk rhythm, or a country "chicken-pickin'" rhythm? Or a big-band horn lick? A walking acoustic jazz bass line? All of these are available for purchase.

WHERE TO FIND LOOPS

Most of the DAWs (Cubase, Logic, Pro Tools, GarageBand, Sequel) come prepackaged with loops, as do most keyboard workstations. They can use each other's loops interchangeably. Sequel by Steinberg, for $80, comes with 5,000 loops, which you can use in any other program. Stylus RMX is wonderful for percussion loops.

Here's the loop browser in Cubase.

FIG 6.2. Loop Browser in Cubase

My go-to commercial loop library is Big Fish Audio. It's one of my favorite resources for loops. The Big Fish Audio site lets you browse loops by genre (rock, heavy metal, country, etc.), by instrument, by speed, or by key. That's my go-to aggregator site for a bunch of loop companies. Sony has a tremendous loop library (www.sonycreativesoftware.com/loops). But you can get most of their products from Big Fish Audio.

Several virtual instruments come with tons of loops. The big player is Toontrack with EZDrummer, where you can get different drum kits with prepackaged loops. For example, you can get the Americana kit, or Heavy Metal, or NY Drums. EZDrummer is the little brother of their Superior Drummer line, which has more kits, more professional sounds, and more loops you can add to your library. In your DAW, you load the virtual instrument, and then use the EZDrummer portal to drag the 2-, 4-, or 8-bar phrase into your project.

You can mix and match these drum loops themselves with different kits. For instance, you might find a great rock groove but play it on a jazz cocktail kit. Similarly, you might choose a bass drum pattern from one loop and a snare hit from another loop library, and a ride from another still. This gives you tremendous flexibility to create your own sound. That's a big leap forward.

More of my favorites: BFD is a drum program, Kontakt has great virtual instruments, Propellerhead has virtual instruments that come with loops. You drag and drop them into your project.

Some virtual instruments generate loops. One such instrument is Stylus RMX, made by Spectrasonics. Stylus RMX is a percussion loop program that contains wonderful stylistic percussion loops: pop, hip-hop, etc.

Be aware, though, that many people have that program and are using the same loops. So, if you are using loops for final recordings, there is the risk that you'll come to the party wearing the same prom dress as another songwriter. The savvy singer-songwriter will therefore modify the loops, customizing them to each project to make them seem unique.

Loop-processing programs are becoming increasingly user-friendly. While in the past you might have had to buy that "Rock Loop at 100 BPM," now, the package will contain the full drum loop (bass, snare, hi-hat, cymbal) and the individual parts as well. This makes it easier to mix and match different parts from different libraries.

When you buy loops, they are generally organized by keys and identified by some kind of arranging moniker, such as "verse."

You can be limited by tempo, particularly for audio loops. They might be called "funky drum loop at 120 bpm." That means that optimally, the beat would be used in a project that is 120 bpm. Some software programs allow you to manipulate—or even automatically adjust—the speed of the audio file to be slower or faster. But depending on how much you slow it down or speed it up, the loop might degrade in quality and start to sound unnatural. This might be a desirable effect, but it might also be a limitation of that particular loop.

So, there are many loops available, in many styles and for many instruments. Rather than hiring live musicians, you're essentially hiring a live musician as a loop.

WORKING WITH LOOPS

Once you have your loop library in your hot little hands, there are several tricks to getting the most out it. For example, you can cut segments of a longer loop into smaller pieces. You don't have to use an entire four-bar or eight-bar string loop. Maybe two bars of it will do.

(a) Complete

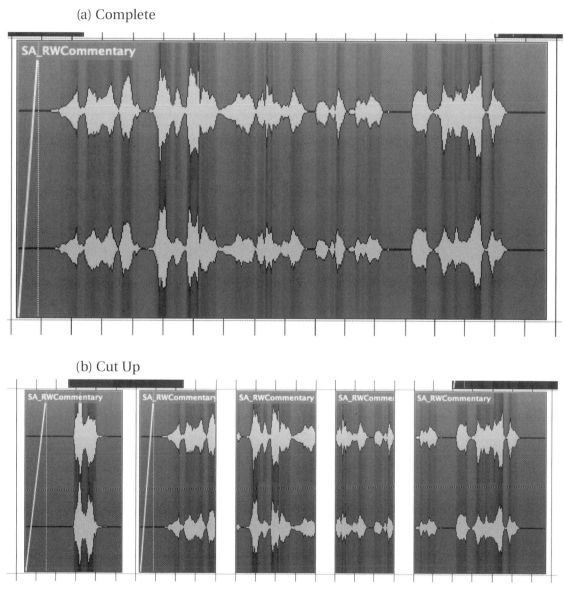

(b) Cut Up

FIG. 6.3. Audio Loop (a) Complete (b) Cut Up

You can also mix and match different loops to create your own orchestral moments. For example, use bar 1 of one loop, bars 2 to 4 of a different loop, bar 5 of another, and bars 6, 7, and 8 of still another. And you don't have to keep them in order! For example, connect bar 3 of loop 1 with bar 7 of loop 2. If it sounds good, it *is* good! With practice and a good ear, you can create very elaborate custom arrangements.

One danger of having too many loops at your disposal is that you might start spending too much time searching for the "perfect" loop instead of knuckling down and actually creating music. Be very careful. I want to throw out the idea that instead of looking for the "perfect" loop, you should look for the "good enough" loop. Here's my feeling on the subject: if you truly want something specific, then hire a real musician to play it.

If I'm stuck for ideas and have some free time, I'll often do what I call "kitchen sink arranging." I'll go through different loop folders. As I preview loops for my project, I'll put several of the "good enough" loops into the mix until I have a cacophony of background parts. I essentially put a ton of ideas up on the screen knowing that I'm going to eventually get rid of most of it, but I'd rather be listening and eliminating than searching and searching and not getting anything recorded. I've usually settled on the drum/percussion groove by this point. Maybe I'll have a verse with a couple layers of rhythm guitar, maybe some horn hits (or other background parts), some strings, and a couple of looped options. I also like to throw in weird, world instrument parts. (These may or may not make the actual mix, but I have them there.)

U2 did this process on their *Joshua Tree* album. They had a *ton* more instruments and instrumentations than what actually made it to the album. There were lots and lots of tracks of random ideas, and then they pared back elements to see what sounded cool. Most of it was thrown away, but what remained was great—a classic album.

You can't always record like this, but if you have some time, and aren't quite sure "what" you want, it's a great way to experiment.

As I mentioned, it's also fun to start writing a song by using a loop. I like to construct little chord progressions using a loop library, and then write to it. It's a different mindset from when I'm playing the part myself. When I'm writing a melody, having my own, little, personal rhythm guitarist on deck is really nice. It lets me focus on using a different part of my brain, and I get different kinds of ideas really quickly using loops, rather than relying on my own playing.

You can use a loop as your click track, or as your metronome.

Sometimes, my loop tracks eventually get replaced with a track by a live player. Especially in the songwriting process, I'll use a loop just to get the idea down. They are useful in my trial-and-error process to find the right tempo, to slow it down or speed it up, without having to go through the expense of having a live drummer trying to figure it out.

AUDITIONING LOOPS

On several occasions, I've done loop purchase binges. One year, I decided I didn't have enough rhythm guitar parts. So, I bought maybe thirty DVDs. All of a sudden, it was completely daunting, with my new pile of a bazillion loops! So, I started auditioning them, with the idea that I'd create favorites to go back to later on, but I found that I never actually did that.

Now, I pretty much only do that when I have a project where I need a loop. You can tell within the first couple seconds whether it will be usable or not.

Many DAWs let you audition a loop before you commit to it. This is a little different than starting the songwriting process with a loop. You can then scroll through candidate loops and audition them against the actual track.

If you're using the loop as a starting point, you're waiting for that magic moment, where the loops will jump up and say, "Hey, take me to the prom!" This can be fun, especially if you are going through loops in a style of music that you can't play. It's really joyful for me. Like, I wish I was king of the strummers, but I'm not, so being able to go through someone playing a series of really wonderfully recorded Telecaster rhythm guitar parts is truly a great pleasure.

Loops in Templates

I created a template of the I VI IV V chord pattern—all the permutations of I VI IV V, grouped into the six ways you can play it starting on the I chord, the six ways you can play it starting on the VI chord, and the six ways you can play it starting on the V chord. There are a bazillion songs that use that chord progression. If I am completely out of song ideas, but I still want to write something, I can pull up this template, and have the arpeggiator, and the pre-set drum pattern, in these different chord changes.

In this and other template files, I preloaded several virtual instruments: a track of Stylus RMX, a track of EZDrummer or Superior Drummer, ready for me to add MIDI loops. I also set up a couple of audio tracks that are ready for me to drag audio loops into.

Having the loops available like this makes the setup very easy. I don't have to go through the whole recording process before I start writing. I can just copy and paste sections of the song. I might set up an entire verse that's all I VI IV V, which could be a two-bar pattern, and then have a two-bar pattern of I VI V IV, and then a two-bar pattern of I IV VI V, and a two-bar pattern of I IV V VI. I just grab these two-bar sections, put them in, and create a song really, really quickly.

Having them based on loops makes that construction process super fast, because I don't have to perform and record them every time I want to create a song.

All of the DAWs have some type of marker track, where you can assign numbers to different parts of the song, so you can quickly navigate to different sections. You can assign marker 1 to the intro, 2 to verse 1, and when you hit 1 on the keyboard, the cursor automatically goes to the section.

Some DAWs have an "arrangement track," where you can select a certain portion of your performance. It's very similar to selecting a loop. Let's say I play a chord pattern for a couple measures. I can then select that chord progression, similar to a marker. I select the beginning and the end of it, and then I can tell the computer program to repeat that. So I'll say, "Repeat measures 1–8 four times, and then play measures 9–16 four times." The DAW will show it repeating those measures, but what you're hearing comes across as an actual section. This allows you to arrange songs very quickly.

Once the loops are installed, the DAW will let you fill out the song sections, using the loops. It's called "flattening" in Cubase; the computer renders that particular arrangement linearly. Instead of playing the loops back as repeats, it plays them back as the complete performance. That allows you to try out different chord progressions. Let's say you're alternating back and forth between a C and an F chord, so your pattern goes "C, F, C, F, C, F, C, F." You decide that for the fourth time, you want F minor instead of F major. You can create a two-bar phrase of C and F minor for that spot (or whatever chord you want). The computer will play "C, F, C, F, C, F." Then, for the last two measures, the computer will grab the F minor loop, and then return to the original arrangement. This allows you to create variations quickly. And since you're using MIDI loops and audio loops, you're hearing it with a whole band arrangement, rather than just you playing it out on the keyboard or the guitar.

This lets you hear bigger versions of your ideas right away. Then, just drag whichever variation you like back into your arrangement, and move on to the next section.

This approach can be very handy. I like programs that help me work faster, and where I'm doing that much programming, I'm doing more playing. Having the audio and the MIDI loops available makes it much easier to create arrangements, and to hear your songs.

Audio loops are limited to certain chords. So, if you're a songwriter that uses quirky chord patterns, sometimes you cannot find loops to facilitate those chord patterns. Also, knowing where to place the loops within a mix can be a little daunting. We'll solve that in later chapters.

LAYERING LOOPS

Loops are utilized in a way similar to multitracked live instruments, except that the parts are already recorded.

Sometimes, there are timing issues between different loops. For instance, a rhythm guitar might be grooving with natural timing variances—the "human" feel of a guitar, which might not align with the precise timing of a quantized beat. You could ask a live musician to adjust to another player, whereas with the loop, you're stuck with what you have. In a DAW, you could adjust those issues.

Another solution is to buy a different loop that better fits the rhythmic timing of your project, because most people don't have the patience or the wherewithal to actually program, cut up, slice, and reposition different portions of an audio loop to make it fit something.

OTHER LOOP GENERATORS

Arpeggiators

An *arpeggiator* is a device that creates loops on the fly, which you can easily adjust and transpose. Many keyboards come with arpeggiators, which you can use with different sounds. Some of the DAWs also have internal arpeggiators. An arpeggiator is like a MIDI version of a guitar strum, or synth pattern, created on the spot based on what chords you're playing. So, you can play a C triad on the keyboard, and it will play an arpeggiated pattern of those notes. If you change chords, the arpeggio pattern will smoothly change chords to fit the notes of your new chord. You don't have to play out all those MIDI notes; just play the chord once, and the exact note and pattern selection happens for you automatically, in the background. In the audio loops, you are limited to what was recorded for you, which can be limiting if you want to use an obscure chord. But the arpeggiator can perform whatever notes you play.

So, the arpeggiated loop is created live, as you play it. The MIDI loop is something you'd drag and drop into a project.

There can be hundreds of these arpeggiated loop patterns to choose from, and this can be daunting. It can also be really fun and bring a different element to your playing.

A practical example, I was doing a funk tune for a project, and found a great Stevie Wonder-esque clavichord part, which I never could have played in a million years, due to my own physical limitations as a pianist. It was far cooler than whatever I could come up with. I only had to play the chord progression, and the arpeggiator took care of all that funky clavinetteness. It was very handy, and I was able to do it very quickly. Normally, I would have hired out a keyboard player who was adept at playing clavichord parts. But this time, it actually worked out just fine, using the arpeggiator.

Arranger Keyboards

Arranger keyboards fulfill the same function as a DAW. Instead of recording to a computer, you record internally, inside the keyboard. Some have touch screens and let you do elaborate arrangements. Initially, you are limited to the internal sounds of that keyboard, though you might be able to export the MIDI file to a DAW and then use your own MIDI sounds.

The three major keyboard brands are Korg, Roland, and Yamaha. They are always in a constant battle to see who has the biggest, baddest, coolest sounds. I'm personally a fan of Yamaha products, but I wouldn't turn up my nose at the other two. At the high end, Roland has the Fantom line, Yamaha has the Motif line, and Korg has the Triton series. They all come prepackaged with loops and arpeggiators and a lot of features, such as internal recording capabilities and connectivity with a DAW. Korgs sometimes have physical vacuum tubes to make the sounds warmer.

The three companies also have consumer grade arranger keyboards with a lot of the same functions, and the sounds are really good, but they are missing some functionality and have fewer sound banks and loops, compared to a DAW. But even on the cheap keyboards, you can do a lot of stuff. To a lesser extent, Casio has some inexpensive, but good keyboards.

Virtual instruments make some of the features of higher-end keyboards a bit redundant. A disadvantage of arranger keyboards is the less powerful editing capabilities. You have a lot more flexibility within a DAW.

When you buy a DAW, it may come with many usable instrument sounds. For instance, if you buy Cubase, it comes prepackaged with all the Motif sounds. For a five/six hundred-dollar program, you're getting a thousand dollars worth of sounds already. I personally tend to lean towards virtual instruments, rather than just what my current keyboard has, because the ones inside my computer are more portable. But one advantage of the keyboard workstations—especially if you're doing a lot of live stuff—is that you can take just the keyboard to the gig. You don't have to carry a laptop with you; you don't have to carry all that other junk with you. You can do it right from the keyboard and press Play.

Software Loop Generators

There are also stand-alone programs that let you program patterns and have some of their own sounds. They are of various quality and cost levels. Programs such as Band-in-a-Box allow you to get into song creation rather cheaply and easily, and they have different strengths. To me, Band-in-a-Box has some strong capabilities towards sketching out arrangements and letting you punch in more sophisticated chord progressions than some tools. Sometimes, the simple programs allow you to work really quickly. Their limitations can actually be an advantage, because you don't have a lot of choices.

A FINAL THOUGHT ABOUT LOOPS

Loops are a great, unsung hero of contemporary music production. Some people look down on loops, because they replace the use of live musicians. I find that loops can be extremely liberating, because a lot of people don't have access to those live musicians. Loops can be a really great writing help, and I'm a huge proponent of them, though I don't use them all the time. I'm lucky, because I have access to great live musicians, and so I probably lean towards using live musicians, when I can. But for those quick and dirty arrangements, I love using loops.

CHAPTER 7

Editing

Once you've got your tracks recorded, you can edit them to create ideal performances. Then, you mix. You might continue editing during mixing, but you try to get them as good as you can beforehand.

CUTTING AND PASTING TRACKS

Cutting and pasting your audio and MIDI tracks is as easy as cutting and pasting text in a computer document. This makes audio editing extremely easy. This form of editing is also non-destructive, meaning if you make a mistake, you can undo the mistake and try again. Every DAW has a cut, copy, and paste tool. They will often look like a pair of scissors, a stamp, and a bottle of glue.

FIG. 7.1. Cut, Copy, and Paste Tools

VOLUME AUTOMATION

Adjusting the volume of individual tracks is a key component to mixing. Some instruments require being softer in some places of the mix, and louder in others. For example, maybe you want a rhythm guitar to be louder in the intro, but softer in the background when the vocalist starts singing the verse. Fortunately, DAWs have what are called automation lanes or automation tracks where you can "draw" in the amount of volume you require at any given moment of the song. You can also draw in swells, and/or create fade-ins and fade-outs on individual instruments.

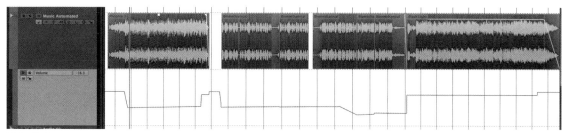

FIG. 7.2. Automation Lane

There are two steps to creating automation for a track. Step one, select the parameter of the track you want to automate; in this example we're selecting volume. This is usually some kind of dropdown menu. Consult the documentation of your DAW on how to open the menu. Selecting the parameter will create an automation lane, usually below your main track.

Step two, on your DAW track, look for an R and W button grouped together. Typically the R is green and the W is red. The "R" stands for "Read Automation," and the "W" stands for "Write Automation."

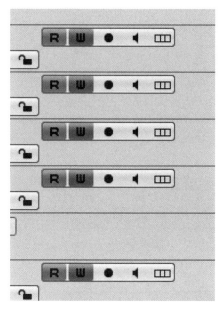

FIG. 7.3. Read and Write Automation Buttons

Select the "W" (the "Write Automation" button) to engage the ability to create automation. On some DAWs a "Draw tool" (often in the form of a pen or pencil) will appear when you hover with your cursor over the automation track, allowing you to immediately draw in your automation. Some DAWs require you to select a "Draw" tool first, and *then* draw your automation. Either way, you still must select the "W."

In addition to drawing your automation, when the "Write Automation" button is engaged, you also can move the fader during playback of the track, and the automation track will record this movement. (This is true of any parameter on the track you are playing back.) In other words, with the "W" engaged, you can record the movement of any adjustable parameter on a track, such as Pan settings, EQ settings, etc. (This includes parameters on plug-ins, which we'll talk about in chapter 8.)

After recording your automation, deselect the "W" and select the "Read Automation" button (the green "R" button), and your DAW will play back your adjustments. To disengage the automation, simply deselect the "R" button.

COMPING TRACKS

When recording an individual track, you don't need to capture a perfect performance from beginning to end. Instead, we can record several "takes," and then piece together the best parts of those takes to create a final version—a "best of" composite take! This process is called "comping tracks."

Comping most commonly occurs on individual vocal parts and solo instrumental parts. Let's say you need to record yourself singing a four-line verse. You breeze through lines 1, 2, and 3, but mess up the melody of line 4. Instead of scrapping the entire performance, you can go back and record multiple passes of line 4 and then choose the best pass. In a pinch, you can even comp a small part of a phrase or even individual words.

There are various common ways to keep track of the tracks used in comping. One way is the lyric sheet, as the vocalist is singing. You put a little marking "take 1, yes," "take 2, no," "take 3, yes," and so on, on the lyric sheet. Cubase supports comping tracks via a feature called "lanes," like freeway lanes. Electronically, you're viewing the different parts that you can combine later.

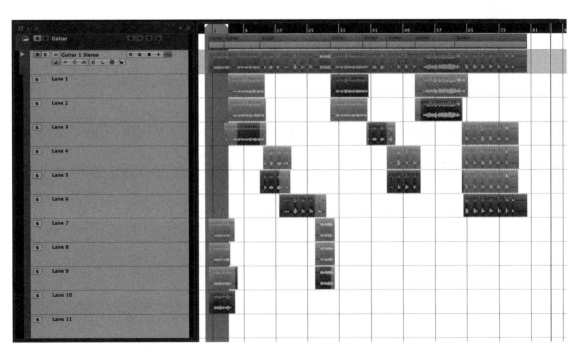

FIG. 7.4. Comping Tracks

Some DAWs allow you to comp within a single track. Other DAWs require you to record multiple tracks to comp. For consistency, try to comp tracks from the same recording session.

TRACK DOCUMENTATION

It's important to keep your takes organized. In a project early in my career, I recorded a guitarist in my studio. He was playing a song's outro, and had complete freedom to try whatever he wanted. We had extra studio time, and we recorded approximately twenty takes at the session—not because he was terrible, but because he was experimenting. Some of his ideas were shorter, some were a little longer, some takes were more chordal, some were more linear.

Being green to the process, I made the mistake of not cataloging which of the guitarist's takes I especially liked. Later, when I came back to that project, I had to go through all twenty takes! In a perfect world, I would have written words like "chordal" or "linear" on the tracks—some kind of guideline to make it easier for me to categorize what he was playing. But I did not do that, and thus created a lot more work for myself. Maintaining a take sheet during the session would have made that easier.

Most DAWs have some kind of electronic note-taking function where you can input what type of microphone you're using, its position, and the mic-pre. You can also make notes about takes there, such as "delete track" or "use take 5." Anything you can do to make mixing easier later on is well worth the couple seconds it takes to put in those extra notations.

Careful, thoughtful notes during the session will help you later on.

OVERDUBBING

Overdubbing is the process of recording over an existing track or set of tracks. There are two ways the term is used. First, you might initially record the rhythm section and then overdub the other instruments. The other common usage of "overdub" is to mean a musician rerecording over an existing part, either to correct a mistake or to try something new (as in comping).

Overdubbing over Rhythm Tracks

"Rhythm tracks" refers to drums, bass, and the guitar parts (and sometimes the piano). These instruments form the foundation of most recordings and are usually recorded first. It is also helpful to have a vocalist sing along on an additional track as a reference for the band, giving them something to play against. This vocal track is called a "scratch vocal" and is typically replaced later. Then, you can overdub additional instruments later on that weren't a part of the original session. This could be a pad, a string part, a solo violin, mandolin, tambourine, synth, and/or other electric guitars. In my sessions, I often have the guitar player come back and rerecord all the guitar parts just so we can get intricate things, or mess around with amp sounds, etc.

When overdubbing, it is easy to end up with a multitude of takes for the same instrument. I've seen sessions with thirty to forty vocal and guitar takes. Try to limit yourself to keeping just three or four takes. There's no need to keep everything you've recorded. Let your ear guide you as to what is keepable, and non-keepable. Again, take extensive notes per take. In fact there's a great book, *Music Industry Forms*, by Jonathan Feist (Berklee Press), that has some really wonderful forms on keeping track of what takes to use and where you can track precise timings; indicating that you might use minutes 1:00 through 1:30 of the vocal, take 1—that kind of thing.

I have a clipboard for paper take sheets. That way, I can write things really quickly. At the end of a session, I type my notes into the relevant track of my DAW. For instance, I document the type of microphone and EQ settings for a vocalist, the best takes, the guitar settings, the amp settings, rough microphone placement, microphone preamp settings, etc. I'll include any notes pertinent to the track that might be helpful later on. Some studios keep a running record on a computer spreadsheet; others use Google Docs and share the information with various people connected to the project. Whether in the track notes of a DAW or a Google Document, it is always better to have the information recorded somewhere.

Overdubbing Multiple Takes

Overdubbing to redo a part happens a lot. You might have an instrumentalist who is struggling to play a lick—either to correct a mistake, or as a kind of discovery process to create a part that works. To help the artist out, you can give them multiple opportunities to record it. You can loop a section, often a four- or eight-bar section, and have them play their part over and over and over again until they finally get it.

I just did a really wonderful session with multiple GRAMMY-nominated artist, Molly Cherryholmes. Her takes were all so good, but she would say after each one, "No, no I need to change that." I just let her do it, even though to me, each take was really astounding. But sure enough, she would do something that would add a little more life to a moment in the song. It's a real joy when you have those types of instrumentalists, and overdubbing may help them to find their best work. We assembled her final cut from several different takes. The beginning, middle, and end were all comped from different takes, where she tried out different ideas.

FIG. 7.5. Molly Cherryholmes

There's a guitar player I often work with named Frank DeBretti who does the same thing. His first takes are always really brilliant, and I'm ready to move on. But he'll say, "Oh no, no let me try this one thing." And he'll play something even more amazing.

FIG. 7.6. Frank DeBretti

You will typically record several different takes with vocalists. I will do three passes through the entire song with the vocalist, having them sing the whole thing. Then, we go back and catch different sections: sing the verse a couple times, sing the chorus a couple times. Then, I will assemble a final take from those different performances. That's one of the beauties of being able to multitrack and overdub.

Overdubbing for Corrections: Punching In and Out

Often, you'll have a beautiful take except for one or two notes. This happens even with the best players. Part of the overdubbing process is going back and fixing just those notes. This is called punching in and punching out. *Punching in* is where you start recording the overdub; *punching out* is where you stop recording it.

Digital audio workstations make punching in and out fairly simple. If possible, start by looking for a natural place for the artist to come in and go out. Since it's all digital, you can bring them in and out much sooner than you actually need or will use, and then adjust the punch later. Sometimes, depending on the project, it's not that easy. But again, make them feel as comfortable as possible doing that.

Be careful of the vocalist changing their position in relation to the mic between overdubs. We've talked about this in chapter 3, about mic technique. I try to get all overdubbing for a single song done on the same day and at the same time, rather than spreading it out. The studio might sound different on different days, so this will help you to have consistency in the recording.

EDITING STRAY SOUNDS

You can also edit out things like people sneezing, chairs banging around in the background, and other extraneous noise. How much of this you do will depend on how pristine you want your mix. Some people fall into the trap of feeling that it needs to be completely pristine, but removing everything can also mean that there is no personality in the track. Sometimes, the person you are recording will bump a music stand, or you'll hear them tap their foot. You have to decide how much it detracts. Some people don't like the sound of finger noise on an acoustic guitar, so they try to eliminate it. Others don't like the sound of breaths.

Personally, I often like those little mistakes because it makes it sound "real." I've had artists scooch in their chair or on the stool, and if it's occurring in a place where there's no music, that's very easy to edit out. Sometimes, you can EQ things like that out, but sometimes, the performance is so good, I'll just leave it in and try to minimize it.

For bigger issues, like a true mistake in the performance, you sometimes have to cut and paste material from different parts of the track. That's one of the wonderful, magical aspects of a digital recording: to be able to move material around easily and quickly.

For instance, I had a rhythm guitar player come in, and he did a really quick session. He decided to play a different rhythm part on a song's second chorus. We really didn't catch how cool it was during the session, but in mixing, we decided to use it also for the first chorus. Just by copying and pasting it, we really improved the track. We couldn't have done that in an era of tape recordings. So, I feel I always have a level of flexibility. I've pasted together solos where none existed, and I've created background parts where none existed simply by cutting and pasting.

PITCH CORRECTION

Pitch correction is another ubiquitous contemporary practice during mixing. I love pitch correction. My philosophy is that I try to get the best performance out of somebody, and then I can use pitch correction tools to fix the little nuances, if they're a little flat or sharp.

Too much pitch correction can make a performance sound unnatural, which may or may not be the actual goal. I personally like the pitch correction to be transparent, meaning that you can't tell that anything was pitch corrected. It takes a level of expertise and practice, but I'm a fan of pitch correction for this purpose.

Typically, pitch correction is done before mixing. After assembling a vocal performance, pitch-correct it, and then bounce it to a new track, which is what you will use when you mix.

Besides adjusting flat or sharp notes, you can use it to actually change performances. We did an acoustic record where we recorded the mandolin part fairly early in the process. Once we started adding some of the other instruments, that early mandolin part didn't quite fit, but I was able to go in and use pitch correction, changing some of the pitches to different notes. He wasn't out of tune; they just sounded like the wrong notes because the tune had evolved. That was really handy, rather than having him come back and record again.

Pitch correction is a way of life. I don't think you can avoid it. The application of pitch correction can vary from making a vocal natural, where the pitch correction is unnoticeable, to what's called the T-Pain effect, where the pitch correction is very prominent and electronic sounding.

There are several different pitch correction software programs. The major players are Auto-Tune and Melodyne. Some DAWs have built-in pitch correction. I use the built-in Cubase pitch correction for my background vocals and for quick corrections on easy "fixes." For lead vocals, I use Melodyne, but Auto-Tune also works great. I personally like a vocal to sound as natural as possible, but others use pitch correction as part of the performance. It's an aesthetic choice.

A hidden function in most pitch correction tools is that you can move the notes linearly, meaning that you can move the notes to a new starting point. Say a singer comes in late on a certain note; you can take that note and you can drag it forward so that it occurs on the correct beat. I did a string section where a young violin player was off just a little bit; not bad, but it was enough to disrupt the flow of the other parts, so I went through and dragged all of his notes to where they matched the bowing attacks of the other players.

You can also use pitch correction to adjust the rate of vibrato. Sometimes by reducing vibrato down to 80 percent, it will make a part fit within the mix a little better. As always, use your ear as your guide. Just because you can do something doesn't mean you *should* do something.

One of my secrets to keeping a vocal sounding natural when using pitch correction is to do as little adjustment as possible when the singing comes in on the attack of the note, because the attack is where listeners identify the characteristic sound of a voice the most. On the attack, I might adjust the pitch where they come in, but I won't touch the vibrato. Some vocalists slide into a note, which may not be perfect, but it sounds natural. I'll cut a note just after the slide and adjust the pitch and vibrato after the initial attack. I find on my mixes, most the time, it's very hard to tell that I've actually done any vocal processing when there actually might be quite a bit.

Adjusting pitch, moving a note linearly, and adjusting vibrato are the biggest tools of pitch correction.

FIXING TIMING

In addition to correcting pitch, you can also fix rhythms and timing—that is, you can *quantize* the recording to the actual exact beat of the music. You can move the attack point of the note closer to the actual beat. If a singer comes in early or a guitar strums late, you can push that file or push that attack to match the beat. It is very common with drum parts to drag the kick drum to where it falls directly on the beat. Where the human drummer may not be perfect, you can make things perfect.

You can do this by moving individual segments of a track, one at a time. In addition, many DAWs let you adjust the time overall, and by various degrees. Instead of having everything perfectly in time, you can select a ratio of time, thus retaining some of the human feel so that it doesn't sound robotic.

CROSSFADES

Whether it's by overdubbing, comping tracks, or punching in and out, when you assemble these fragments of tracks together, you *crossfade* between the two sounds to smooth the transition between cuts: where one volume gradually increases while the other gradually decreases. This makes the edit smoother, rather than an abrupt cut. It's almost instantaneous—we're talking milliseconds—but without these smooth transitions, our ears will pick up those little annoying breaks at the edit.

(a) Without Crossfade

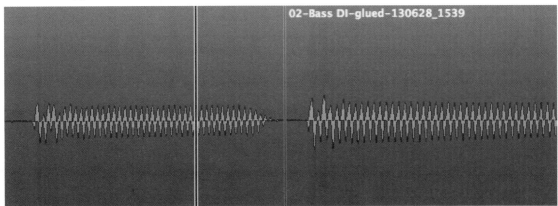

(b) With Crossfade

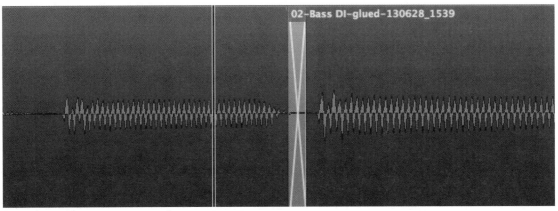

FIG. 7.7. Adding a Crossfade (a) Without Crossfade (b) With Crossfade

ARRANGING DURING MIXING

Many beginning recordists fall into the trap of thinking that they must use everything they record, or must use a recorded instrument constantly throughout a track. That's simply not the case. I tend to work back from the vocal, taking parts out at the beginning and then adding more instruments as the track progresses.

If you want your choruses to sound more dynamic, you might take out instrumentation in the verses. Let's say you have two acoustic guitar parts. One is a solo part that's just kind of noodling lines, and one is more strumming. I might take out the strumming guitar completely in the verses so that when the choruses come in, the band's sound has more body.

The density of instrumentation gives a perception of loudness. The chorus might sound louder, even though it is not actually louder, just because more instruments are playing there. You'll hear this a lot in EDM (electronic dance music), where they're really wonderful with using space to create a spatial arrangement. And so, it's not just one loud sound, or just one quiet sound, throughout the whole piece.

A good arranger can figure this all out before a session, but it is also common to make these decisions in mixing.

CHAPTER 8

Mixing

In mixing, we place all our different recorded tracks together and try to make them sound good as a unit. It is part magic, part art, and part science.

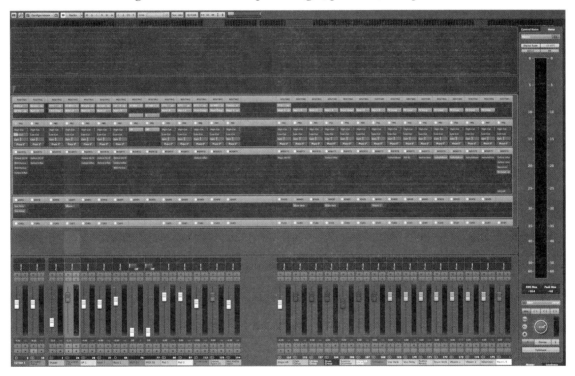

FIG. 8.1. DAW Mixing Board

There's a difference between a good recording level and what sounds good in a mix. When you record, the goal is to capture each instrument at its best, using the ideal mic for that instrument and getting a good recording level on the track. When you put the different individual recordings together, you'll find that different instruments will be at different levels within your mix, and not a sonic relationship that sounds natural. Your primary job when mixing is to achieve a pleasing balance between all the recorded instruments.

Additionally, you might have, say, a vocalist who sings some parts softly and some of them loudly, within the recording. When you mix it, you might have to raise the level of the soft parts and lower the level of the loud parts so that it all sounds consistent. If the vocals are soft and an electric guitar comes in loud, you might not be able to hear the vocals. So, in mixing, you would raise the vocals up, or perhaps lower the louder guitar.

Once the relative levels are set, the goal becomes to make the band sound natural, with the same relationships that we would find in a real performance.

If you observe a live, acoustic performance on stage, typically, the singer is in the middle. There might be a drummer behind the singer, a guitar player to the singer's left, and a bass player to the singer's right. That arrangement will give the band a good sound.

In a mix, to capture that natural arrangement, you need to recreate how the musicians are positioned on stage. The drums should sound like they're behind the singer, the guitarist should be a little bit to the left, and the bass player should be a little bit to the right and a little bit behind the singer.

To achieve this illusion, we have three basic dimensions of the sound we can adjust:

1. Stereo field, left and right (panning)

2. Frequency range, low to high (EQ)

3. Depth of field, front to back (reverb and delay)

Mixing is a process of adjusting these three dimensions in order to create a great sounding recording.

FREQUENCY RANGE

The goal of working with frequencies is to make each instrument fit in its ideal frequency range without overlapping other instruments.

Every instrument has a frequency range. *Frequency* is where the sound of an instrument takes up space in the spectrum between, and including, low-to-high frequencies. For example, when strumming a guitar, the sound of the pick scraping across the strings creates a high frequency, the vibrating strings themselves are in the medium frequency range, and the strings vibrating through the wood of the guitar are in the lower frequencies. This may sound great for solo guitar, but when you add other instruments that share those same frequencies, the shared frequencies will be unnaturally boosted in the recording, creating a muddy mix. When your panning is set, you can further clarify the band's sound by adjusting the frequencies of each track.

For any instrument, some frequencies will sound good and others won't. Additionally, the frequencies of different instruments may overlap. When mixing, you can remove, reduce, or (less often) boost these frequencies of the different instruments to help them sound better as an ensemble.

Imagine an instrument's sound as six blocks stacked on top of each other. Within each frequency range, I'm going to use my EQ controls to take away problematic frequencies. You usually don't boost frequencies; more often, you take them away.

Mix engineers argue about this frequency range, but the following chart shows my opinion on the five main frequency areas to balance out when you are mixing multiple instruments.

High Frequencies	**6 kHz – 20 kHz**
	Brightness/crispness
	Not enough is dull or flat
	Too much 6 kHz – 8 kHz is sibilant
	Too much 8 kHz – 16 kHz is brittle
	Sensed more than heard above 16 kHz
High Midrange	**4 kHz – 6 kHz**
	Clarity and definition
	Boost to bring forward in mix
	Cut to reduce sibilance
	2 kHz – 4 kHz
	Percussive attack
	Vocal recognition
	Hard consonants
	Too much can bring on listener fatigue
Midrange	**250 Hz – 2 kHz**
	Low-order harmonics of most instruments
	Too much 500 Hz – 1 kHz can be honking
	Too much 1 kHz – 2 kHz can be tinny
Bass	**60 Hz – 250 Hz**
	Fundamental notes of rhythm section
	Increase to make sound fatter
	Decrease to make sound thinner
	Too much sounds boomy
Sub Bass	**16 Hz – 60 Hz**
	Sense of power
	Too much is muddy

FIG. 8.2. Frequency Spectrum

I'll usually start by EQing my bass guitar and bass drum. They are fighting for the same low frequencies, so I'll try to reduce where they overlap—usually at around 100 Hz.

Bass drums are usually pitched a little lower than bass guitar, so at 100 Hz, I might cut off the top end of my bass drum and roll off the bottom end of my bass guitar, so that there's no muddy sound where they overlap.

Then, I will work my way up the frequency spectrum, to the other instruments. Guitars and vocals often have some overlap too, in the midrange. I will reduce guitar frequencies so that the vocal will fit, because usually, the vocal is more important than the guitar part.

Typically, I roll off all of the bass frequencies of all my instruments, except for the bass drum and the kick drum. There is no desirable activity down that low in the mid-range instruments, so I eliminate everything 60 Hz and lower. This creates a tighter sounding mix in the low frequencies, with nothing getting in the way of the bass drum and the bass.

FIG. 8.3. EQ Rolling off at 60 Hz

A parametric EQ plug-in lets you adjust different portions of the frequency spectrum. At a basic level, it's low, medium, and high frequencies. If you have a five-band parametric EQ, it might label the different bands low, low-mid, mid, high-mid, and high. There are also seven-band EQs. On the other hand, a simple EQ on a car stereo usually just has a treble and a bass, set to 100 Hz and 1,000 kHz, and can just raise or lower parts of the spectrum. The EQ on your DAW is more nuanced.

On a parametric EQ, you can move where you're going to raise or lower the frequency response. Different voices have sweet spots. Parametric EQs have a *sweepable frequency*, meaning that instead of a predetermined frequency to increase or reduce or lower, you can sweep through to find a specific frequency to adjust. A parametric EQ also allows you to increase or decrease the frequen-cies on either side of your chosen frequency. This is called the "Q" parameter. The Q parameter gives you an option to pinpoint a very narrow single frequency. For instance, if the S sounds your the vocalist sings are whistle-y, you can find and reduce the pitch of the actual whistle without affecting the rest of the "S" sound. Or, let's say the Ts and Ps sung by the vocalist are too boom-y, which indicate multiple frequencies adjacent to where the actual pitch of the "boom" is. You can widen the "Q" to grab as much of the boom as possible without making the rest of the vocal sound thin. You can set the width of the spectrum you are adjusting by using the Q parameter.

Usually, you use EQ to diminish problematic frequencies, rather than emphasizing the sweet spots. A good way to think about it is that you are rolling off the frequencies that are interfering with the sweet spots of other instruments.

Occasionally, you might try and boost a frequency, often in the high range, to get an airy sound. But as I said, for the vast majority of EQing, you're removing frequencies that are getting in the way.

The more instruments in your recording, the more you're going to have to EQ. If you're just doing a guitar/vocal, you will not have to EQ too much because there won't be significant interference. Sometimes, just panning the guitar will reduce any interference between the two. Using good microphones and recording technique also reduces the amount of necessary EQ adjustments.

To help locate problematic frequencies, you can use a spectrometer—available now as a smartphone app. It's like a visual EQ, showing all the different frequencies in a sound. You can play back a spectrometer of a guitar, and then play back a spectrometer of a vocal part, to determine where they're overlapping. But really, the key is to do it by ear and not by sight. The meter might tell you to get rid of more than is really necessary. Always go by how it sounds.

PANNING

Panning is the process of setting each instrument's position in the stereo field, left to right. Once the frequencies are set, I start panning instruments. Usually the low instruments and voice are centered. Then, the higher pitched instruments are placed to the right and left of center.

It's helpful to imagine the stereo field as half a clock face, with twelve o'clock being dead center, three o'clock being full to the right, nine o'clock being fully to left. Typically, the lead vocalist (high-mid frequency) is set at twelve o'clock. Bass guitar and bass drum are there as well. You might pan your acoustic guitar to eleven o'clock, the piano to one o'clock, and then the background vocals to ten o'clock. If you have a male and a female background vocalist, you might put the female at two o'clock and the male at eleven o'clock.

L90	L84	L78	L72	L66	L60	L54	L48	L42	L36	L30	L24	L18	L12	L6	0	R6	R12	R18	R24	R30	R36	R42	R48	R54	R60	R66	R72	R78	R84	R90
9				10 o'clock					11 o'clock						12 o'clock				1 o'clock					2 o'clock						3
Full Left															Center															Full Right

FIG. 8.4. Stereo Panning

Try to balance where things are, left to right, and separate instruments that have similar function and range. Then listen, and see if they are in each other's way. Moving an instrument a little bit to the left or right can clear up some muddiness.

There are many different techniques and opinions about panning, and where to set each instrument. The biggest arguments occur regarding the drum kit. Do you want the kit panned from the drummer's perspective, or the audience perspective? Should the snare be to the left or to the right? Most drummers set the snare a little to their left, but the audience facing them sees it on the right.

Include this panning information in your DAW templates, and then adjust it if you need to.

Panning is often under-utilized by beginning mixers, but it can really make the difference between an adequate mix and a really good mix. So, use that stereo field, and don't be afraid to set instruments at its extreme ends, hard left or hard right.

ADDING PLUG-INS

The next aspect of mixing (depth of field) requires the use of plug-ins. *Plug-ins* are inside-the-computer, audio-processing devices, such as reverbs, delays, compressors, etc. Most DAWs come equipped with their own set of plug-ins. There are also a slew of manufacturers that produce plug-in devices, whether they be completely custom or digital recreations of common and classic hardware devices. Every DAW track will have a series of slots available for single or multiple plug-in placement.

Here are some common plug-ins that come with Cubase. Notice how they graphically model hardware devices.

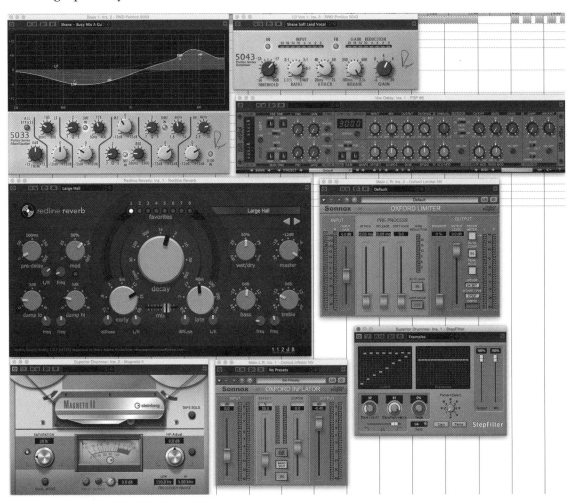

FIG. 8.5. Plug-ins in Cubase

Plug-ins are applied to tracks via the mixing board, and they're called "inserts." Here's how that interface looks in Cubase.

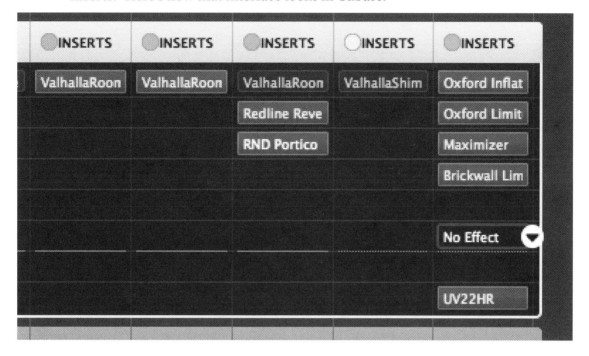

FIG. 8.6. Plug-in Slots on a Track, in Cubase

DEPTH OF FIELD

The third adjustment is depth of field, which we can control by using reverb and delay controls, usually via plug-ins within your DAW. With reverb, you are mimicking either a larger or a smaller space. The short story is that reverb sounds good—but too much sounds bad.

To start using reverb, first imagine the space that you want your band to be playing in. Typically, you're recording in your living room. But would this style of music sound most natural in an amphitheater, or a coffee house, or a rock club? What's the "native habitat" for your music?

Decide on the type of place, and then imagine everything that's going to be in that space. For instance, a rehearsal space is not going to have much in it, so it's going to be a medium reverb space with lots of reflection. A club, though, will have lots of people. Those people are going to absorb some of the lower frequencies, and the higher frequencies tend to zip around. A singer/ songwriter might play in a coffee shop. So, how big is the coffee shop? It might be a medium to large room, fairly reflective because there are lots of tables and chairs. The table-to-people ratio is probably pretty equal, so the tops of those tables are going to be a little more reflective. There might be windows, which are pretty reflective.

My coffee shop singer/songwriter would have a different sound than he/she would playing in a heavy metal room, which is perhaps a smaller club with curtains on the wall—and big, red drapes with pentagrams on them! It's not as live a sound as that reflective coffee shop.

An example of augmenting reverb: I recently recorded a choir here in Nashville in a space that had some natural reverb, but we wanted more. I have a plug-in that has the acoustic space of Notre Dame, and the choir director loves that sound. So I added Notre Dame to the mix, and he was overjoyed.

It's helpful to visualize the actual room and consider the characteristics of the space you are trying to emulate. The more flat objects there are in a space, the more reflective the room is going to sound. If there are more curtains and more people/absorptive flesh, it's going to be less reflective. A stadium with lots of empty seats will be both a large space and very reflective because all of those flip-up stadium seats are going to reflect the sound. If the stadium is full of people, it's going to be a large room but not necessarily that reflective. A coffee house with standing room only might be a medium-sized space with no reflections. But that coffee house with lots of tables and a few customers might be a medium space but more reflective, which might give you a more intimate sound.

Reverb vs. Delay

The two tools to get these different room sounds are reverb and delay, and they are actually degrees of the same thing. The difference between them is a matter of how much you're able to distinguish the reflections. Delay usually means your ear can physically distinguish the reflections (i.e., the echo). Once the echoes all start blending into one another, then the effect becomes a reverb.

(a) Reverb

(b) Delay

FIG. 8.7. Reverb and Delay

With delay, you can add a little bit of reflection without adding muddiness. A trend in pop music is to use delay instead of reverb on the vocals and other acoustic instruments.

Reverbs will add more distortion to the original sound, and also depth—and beautifully so. But delays decrease the amount of muddiness, particularly if you have a lot of instruments.

Using different degrees of these tools places something either far forward or in the back of the mix. The more of either effect you add, the farther away the sound will be perceived to be. For a lead vocalist, since he's at the front of the stage, you may not put a lot of reverb on his voice. It would just muddy him up. The drums, though, are placed further back, so reverb would help to give that impression.

COMPRESSION

FIG. 8.8. Compressor

Compression gives a track more presence and punch. It makes softer parts of a track louder while keeping louder passages of the track unchanged. So, the overall effect is to make the instrument more present in the mix, though not louder overall. You can thus add more of an instrument to a mix without changing the instrument's overall level.

Compression can be used on any instrument, but most commonly, it is used on voice. It can make a voice sound meatier, with more "oomph." It is also commonly used on snare drums to give them a stronger smack.

GROUPING TRACKS

In mixing, sound processing such as compression, EQ, and delay are usually added to individual instruments. Reverb, though, is often applied to groups of tracks so there is an overall uniformity to the sound of the mix. In other words, you want the instruments to sound like they are playing in the same room. You can send multiple instruments into the same reverb by first sending them to the same bus.

Also, sometimes, you might put the other plug-ins on multiple tracks for the same instrument. As discussed in chapter 3, when I record an acoustic guitar, I typically use two or three mics: one that's really close to the front of the guitar, one that's over the player's shoulder, and then sometimes one on the neck of the guitar. Using EQ, reverb, and compression on each of those channels would be too much of a drain on my computer. Instead, I group those three channels into a single channel, called a "bus," and then apply EQ, compression, and reverb to that. It's just three applications of processing, rather than nine, which is much easier on the CPU.

ORDER OF EVENTS

First you do the panning, then you do the EQ. While you're doing the EQ, you're listening to instruments in relationship to each other.

We're discussing these different steps sequentially, but in practice, they are all interlocking. In practice, when you decide to bring in the guitar strumming in the verses, you might then realize that you need to raise the volume of the vocals slightly, and reduce something else. Everything affects everything else.

LOCALIZED ADJUSTMENTS

Panning, reverb, and EQ typically stay the same throughout a track. These are all settings for the whole track all the way through from beginning to end.

However, volume levels may change during the course of a track. To control this, your DAW gives you the capability to "draw in" the relative volume level throughout a track. There's the term "vocal riding." It is like horseback riding, where the mix engineer adjusts the vocals throughout the entire mix as it goes along, raising it and lowering it in increments to give the impression that it has the same volume throughout. As different instruments come in and out of a mix, the changing density of the arrangement falsely makes the lead vocal sound like it's louder or softer. For instance, a guitar playing during the verse or chorus will be relatively soft in relationship to the lead vocal, because the guitar shouldn't crowd out the lyrics. But during the guitar solo, when the voice is absent, the guitar might be too quiet, and so you would raise the level of the guitar during the solo. Then, when the voice comes in, you pull back the sound of the guitar. So, the volume level will move up and down within a track, depending on what's happening in the mix.

I just produced the music for a documentary. The underscore was playing while the subject of the documentary walked down a hallway. He walked to his office, opened the door, and then the door closed. You hear the background music and the live sound of him walking down the hallway at the same time. Well, when he shuts the door, it made this big "clunk" sound, and it just so happens that right at that part of the underscore, there's this little guitar phrase that's quite nice.

I can't make the guitar suddenly loud at that point, then make it soft again. So in the mix, I drew in what looks like a little V shape where the door closed, to reduce the sound of that clunk. I also slightly boosted the guitar part there so the whole sequence sounded smooth and natural.

The same thing with the guitar, I can't just suddenly make the guitar loud and then make it soft again. So, in using a combination of reducing the door slam a little bit, and boosting the guitar just a little bit, it sounds really natural. But if you look at it on the edit screen, you'll see a boost and you'll see a dip.

REFERENCE TRACKS

Usually before we record, we try and find reference tracks that are close to what we're doing in our session. I like to create "soundscapes" with my artists. We'll have five to ten different songs that have elements that they really like. One element might be a certain piano sound, another a certain reverb on the piano. These models can be very helpful.

I had a client last year who plays acoustic guitar, and he had one track that also had acoustic piano. For some reason, we did not do a soundscape on that piano track. And so, the track that I created for him was a very clear, kind of a grand piano sound—a very pretty sound. But he actually wanted more of a rough, slightly detuned piano sound. The track actually did not make it onto the album because we disagreed. If we had discussed what he wanted beforehand, we could have avoided the misunderstanding completely.

Sometimes, though, you can fix these issues in the mix, and try to match your own recording to one of your "soundscape" models. You can import your soundscape into a track on your session, and just switch between that and your own recording. There's even a specific plug-in, AB Mix (by Sample Magic), which helps you to do this. You insert it into a track, which you can then use for your reference with up to nine reference mixes. So from within the mix, instead of having to go to iTunes and then back in, you can load an MP3 or a WAV file of a reference track and have that accessible from your mixer.

The point is, it is very helpful to have a sense of what you're going for before you mix because that's going to help you make choices on your sound process, where you place your instruments in the stereo field, and so on. I always encourage my clients to go with what they like.

You might find it helpful, especially when you are first learning how to mix, to go to a favorite recording, and to attempt to duplicate what you like about it.

CHAPTER 9

Final Steps: Mastering and More

Mastering puts a professional sheen on your finished product. The short explanation of why you should have your mixed tracks mastered is that mastering makes your song sound better. It makes it louder and more present, with more "punch." The most noticeable part of mastering is the process of using compression to make your track louder. However, true mastering engineers will also perform some additional wizardry and witchcraft. For example, they might use EQ to manhandle errant frequencies that might not have gotten out of the mix, or that only become apparent when heard across several songs because of the speakers or headphones used during mixing.

Also during mastering, you can look at several different songs in relationship to each other. If their dynamic range varies wildly, they can be set in the same sonic range during mastering. Then, one song won't sound extremely loud, and then one sounds really soft, and then one's kind of medium. They'll all sound about the same level of loudness—or *perceived* loudness. For this reason, if you're doing an EP or an album, it's best to master them all at the same time.

Ideally, someone different than the mix engineer should master your tracks. The mix engineer has lived with all the mistakes and idiosyncrasies of the track, and there's a tendency to become accustomed to some sonic flaws, such as errant frequencies. So, if you mix it yourself, you should have a fresh set of ears master it. If you have someone else mix it, you could master it, though I'd still recommend hiring a specialized mastering engineer, if you can.

Again, in mastering, you can calm down some of the frequencies in an EQ range. So, let's say you have a lot of mid-rangy instruments. You record a piano, rhythm guitar, and also maybe a baritone singer. The mid-range of those three instruments will build upon each other, and create a false sense of more mids than what you might like. You may not have caught it in the mix, but the mastering engineer can smooth that out, and make it sound better.

Reverb sometimes also plays a role in mastering. While it is usually added in mixing, reverb is sometimes fine-tuned during mastering to make tracks sound more uniform.

There are other plug-ins with pre-sets that can help you in the process. But typically, EQ and compression are the two primary tasks of mastering: they make the end product louder and taming errant frequencies.

TOOLS OF MASTERING

Mastering software and plug-ins are available to accomplish these tasks. They resemble mixing tools, but are calibrated and optimized differently. A "pro-grade" mastering mixer and compressor will have more fine-tuned controls than would a compressor intended for mixing. Technically, you can use a mastering compressor for mixing, or a mixing compressor for mastering. But, for instance, you may want to compress only a certain frequency band, like your highs, or you only want to compress the mids. Mastering compressors are built to facilitate that, where you can either leave out certain frequencies, or only include chosen frequencies to compress, or EQ, for that matter. But it would be awkward to use that during initial tracking.

In a mastering set of devices, whether it's hardware or software, there are usually more fine-tunable controls.

EQ AND COMPRESSION

The most important tools of mastering are a parametric EQ and a compressor. A *parametric EQ* has very small bandwidth, meaning you can select minute pieces of the frequency pie and either augment (boost) them or downplay (cut) them. Same thing with the compressor. You typically run the stereo mix through either a dedicated mastering machine or software tool.

Typically, you will EQ first, and then compress it at the very end of the process. If you're mastering a single, the goal is to make it sound as good as you can. If you're mastering multiple tracks within a project (EP, album, film, etc.), you'll also have to make sure that all the levels match, and so you'll set up an A/B scenario where you can compare the tracks against each other.

You are looking for how the tracks stand out from each other in bad ways. For instance, maybe one song has two many high frequencies. By itself, the mix may sound fine. But let's say you recorded clarinets and flutes, and you have mixed the most beautiful clarinet and flute song in existence known to man. Then, your second song is all timpani and electric bass, and you have mixed the most beautiful timpani and electric bass song in existence. Individually, they sound great, but when you play them back-to-back, the clarinet/flute song might suddenly seem too harsh, and the timpani/bass song might suddenly seem too deep. So, you might pull back on some of the high end on the flute song, and you might downplay some of the bass frequencies of the other, just so they sound good playing back-to-back. Additionally, for the flute/clarinet song, since those instruments are relatively quiet, you might have to compress

them a lot to bring them up to a perceived loudness that matches your bass/
percussion/timpani song. You may not compress the bass/timpani song as
much, so that the listener can have a pleasing experience going from one song
to the next, listening to a unit of songs rather than individual songs.

LOUDNESS

Loudness is a perception of the difference between the loudest signal recorded
and the softest signal. Essentially, compression takes the softer signals and
makes them louder while ignoring the original loud signals on a track. So,
you're reducing the difference between the loud and the soft dynamics.

Let's say you have a very loud passage. If you make it louder, you'll get
distortion, so you're kind of stuck with its level. But, if you have a very soft
passage, compression lets you make just the softer notes louder, without
making the loud signal louder/distorting. Making that soft part louder gives
the impression that the entire recording is louder. So again, you're dealing
with perception.

MASTERING SOFTWARE

Most DAWs come bundled with some type of mastering tools. There are many
third-party plug-ins for mastering, such as excellent ones by Waves and Sonnox
Oxford. Engineers and producers will all have their favorite set of plug-ins, but
most of these tools are doing similar things. As long as you have something,
it will work. Many of the native DAW plug-ins work really, really well. They
sound terrific.

Presets on these tools can be a good starting point for getting a good sound.
A mastering tool might have presets called "Rock Band," "Bright Rock," "Funky
R&B," and so on. You can choose a preset according to the style of music you're
playing and just pick that "mastering chain" of tools to process your track. The
mastering chain is the last step of your song's production, so it's located right
before the last fader on your output. You pull up a preset, and your DAW will
automatically place the compressor, EQ, reverb, and limiter (or whatever series
of plug-ins are spec'd for that preset sound) in the chain. It's very convenient.

Then, you adjust the sounds until you find something that sounds good,
because again, you're entering a territory of personal preference. At a basic
level, it's the loudness issue. Can you make the final mix sound louder? That's
usually pleasing to people, so make it louder.

At some point, you have to turn your multitrack mix into a stereo mix. You
bounce your finished multitrack mix file(s) as stereo AIFF or WAV files, and
then import those either into a fresh new DAW session or a new session in a
mastering environment.

Usually, you will master your tracks using a separate mastering program, in addition to your DAW. Technically, you can master within your DAW, because again, you might be using those same plug-ins. But I recommend getting a dedicated mastering program, such as Steinberg WaveLab or Sony Sound Forge. These are optimized for mastering. You can add compression and EQ, but also do additional end-of-production tasks such as burn CDs or add metadata, such as ISRC codes, song names, information about the songwriter and musicians, production date, and so on. Metadata can also be added with other programs, like iTunes.

MASTERING SPEAKERS

Proper "mastering" speakers are expensive, because they're super transparent. You get exactly what you hear. The speakers don't add any color at all to the audio signal. Prices for pro-level mastering speakers start at around $1,000 per speaker, and better ones can cost $3,000 or $4,000 each. On a budget, the key to achieving the same result is to play the tracks on as many different sound sources as you can. Again, my car is "Studio C." When I'm working with one of my engineer buddies, we'll listen to our tracks in my car, his truck, on an iPhone with earbuds—just as many different formats as we can. Once you get to the point of, "Oh, it sounds really good on everything I'm playing it on," you're finished.

Mastering is also where you put all your fades in your song, set the amount of silence between songs, and determine the order of songs on the album.

SONG ORDER

Another task of mastering an album is to settle the song order. I like my albums to have a dynamic journey, so that there's some movement of that loudness. You might start with a loud song and end with a soft song, just so there's some dynamic movement—so that it's not all one energy level.

Our culture has increasingly moved towards a single-driven listening experience, where people aren't listening to entire records. They buy just a single, rather than a whole album. Still, as an artistic expression, I personally like to have a sonic journey. In fact, when I mix songs that have the same instrumentation, I might EQ them a little bit differently, so that it's not so samey-same over the course of an entire production. I also like to write in a variety of keys, just to get different sonic signatures.

HIRING A MASTERING ENGINEER

It's best if you can hire a mastering engineer. They're typically fairly inexpensive, ranging from $100 to $500 per song. Interestingly, a great mastering engineer will actually be faster, and often cheaper, than a less experienced engineer. A lot of times, you'll end up paying less with a more experienced mastering engineer, because he can zip things through. Erik Wolf here in Nashville is a brilliant mastering engineer, and he's super fast. Jonathan Wyner in Cambridge, MA (M-Works Studios), is another great mastering engineer, and he also teaches at Berklee (and authored the excellent book *Audio Mastering*, published by Berklee Press). So, hiring a top-flight mastering engineer often feels like it should be more expensive than it really is.

FIG. 9.1. M-Works Mastering Studios. Photo courtesy of Jonathan Wyner.

Again, there's a kind of wizardry and magic aspect of mastering. The guys who do mastering all the time are so good at it, and they really can make a huge difference on a track. They can make a mediocre mix sound so much better, and then if they get a great mix, they can really make it shine, absolutely. While I have the basic capabilities of mastering, myself, I would rather spend the extra money and take it to a mastering engineer.

Most mix engineers and mastering engineers choose not to do both stages for their own projects. The mix engineer I use is brilliant and quite capable of mastering, but he doesn't like to master his own projects because he tends to hear the mixes as independent units, whereas the mastering engineer hears the effect of all the tracks in relation to each other.

I recommend, even on demos, having someone else master the final track. Most people can do a really good job on a basic mix, but mastering is harder. A good mastering engineer can really improve a track, beyond just making it louder.

AFTERWORD

The key to getting the most out of your home studio is in being willing to experiment and record a lot. It's been my experience that people have a tendency to want to wait until they're experts until they start to record. So, maybe you bought this book in hopes of becoming an expert. Great! But there's no substitute for just doing it and listening, and having a body of work that grows gradually, rather than all of a sudden flooding the market with your brilliance five years later.

So, record a lot. Many people seem to hate the stuff that they recorded two or three years ago, but then after about six years, they actually grow nostalgic for that older material. Tastes can change, but there's some amazingly "badly recorded" songs that are still great songs and have become huge hits. The magic is in the songwriting, and not necessarily in the drum sound. I know guys that will spend days just trying to get the perfect snare hit, but ultimately, that's not as important as just trying to get the song down, flaws and all. Then, let it live on its own and be what it is in that moment.

My final advice: Don't quit, and work harder than everyone else. There are thousands and thousands of very talented people who do not stick with it. I started from the very, very bottom, and I have dedicated myself to just learning the art—to learning as much as I can.

Try to learn something new every single day. Keep your ears open, listen to great songs, ask a lot of questions, get a lot of advice from people that you respect, and always be happy for other peoples' successes. Music isn't a competition. Someone else's success does not diminish your own potential for success.

In my own career, what I have done better than a lot of people that are much more talented than me, is that I've just simply hung in there. I've stayed in the game, and I've worked in the game, and I genuinely feel like if I can do it, anybody can do it.

If you are not afraid of the work and you put in the necessary time, you'll be able to do it too.

ABOUT THE AUTHOR

Photo by Kelly Blaine

Shane Adams is a twice GRAMMY-nominated music educator and an award-winning producer and songwriter. Shane is president of Artist Accelerator and a founding lyric/ songwriting instructor for Berklee Online, the online education division of Berklee College of Music.

Shane is a featured songwriter and instructor for the Taylor Swift Education Center at the Country Music Hall of Fame and Museum where he received their Top Ten Hitmaker award for 2014. He codeveloped their groundbreaking "Words and Music" curriculum, which has enabled over 100,000 (and counting!) elementary through high school students to learn the craft of songwriting. Shane has served on the Hall of Fame's Museum Expansion Advisory Board and has facilitated other music outreach programs, such as "Poetry in Motion" co-sponsored by the Nashville Arts Commission and the NCAA Women's Final Four.

In 2013, Shane was named the Music Industry Professional of the Year by Chowan University, and in 2005, he earned the Tennessee Songwriter Association International's highest honor, the Hallman Award, for outstanding contributions to the songwriting community.

Shane is currently the featured composer for Fjor Films and has produced the music and scored several independent film projects, including Fortune Cookie (featured at both the Sundance and Hollywood Film Festivals).

Shane is recognized internationally as a groundbreaking songwriting lecturer and music production panelist. He is a regular columnist for iSing Magazine and is co-host/co-producer for iTunes featured podcast, *Studio Soundtrack: Music We Live By.*

Shane Adams is a Las Vegas native, a Berklee College of Music alumnus, and currently resides in Nashville, Tennessee.

INDEX

A

AB Mix plug-ins, 119
absorptive surface, 13–14, 116
acoustic guitar
    direct input and, 53, 54
    microphone and, 54–55
AKG headphones, 7
Alesis microphone inputs, 15
amplifier, 57
    acoustic guitar and, 53
    electric guitar and, 53, 55, 56, *56*
arpeggiator, for loops, 95–96
arrangement track, loops and, 94
arranger keyboard, loops and, 96
audience, songwriter and, 37
audio interface, x, 26. *See also* Musical Instrument
        Digital Interface
    electric guitar and, 56
    FireWire port and, 5, 25
    headphone mixes and, 71
    input ports and, 6
    latency and, 6
    troubleshooting and, 29
    USB port and, 5, 25
audio streaming, ix
Audio-Technica microphones, 5, 49
Auratone speakers, 10
automation lanes, editing and, 98–100, *99*
Auto-Tune pitch correction, 105
Avalon direct injection boxes, 22
Avantone microphones, 5, 49

B

balanced cables, 17
balanced power unit, electricity and, 22–23, *23*
balanced signal, 21
bass guitar, 58
Behringer speakers, 9
Big Fish Audio loops library, 90
Blue microphones, 49
boom stand, microphone and, 19
Brown, Susie, *64*
buffering, 6
busses, 69–70, 118

C

cables, 17
    organization of, 18–19
    snake for, 18
Cherryholmes, Molly, 103, *103*
chord charts, 32, *33*, 36
chorus, 35, 57
clean signal. *See* direct input
click tracks, 36–37
    countoff in, 69
    DAW and, 68
    setup of, *68*
    tempo and, 69
    types of, 68
clipping, 26, 29
comping, 53, 100, *100*
compression, 47, 117, 120
compressor, *117*
computer, 1, 2–3, 25
condenser microphone, 48, 49, 50
countoff, in click tracks, 69
Countryman direct injection boxes, 21
crossfade, 107, *108*
Cubase recording software, 3–4

D

DAW. *See* Digital Audio Workstation
delay, 116–17, *117*
Denbo, Tim, *58*
depth of field. *See* reverb
diaphragm, in microphone, 48
DiBretti, Frank, *55*
Digital Audio Workstation (DAW)
    busses and, 28, 66, 69, 118
    channels and, 27
    click tracks and, 68
    efficiency of, 2
    features of, 3
    headphones and, 66, 70
    main outputs and, 66
    MIDI and, 66, 77, *77*, 85, 87
    mixing and, 66, *91*, 91–92
    Record Enable function on, 27, 28
    shortcuts for, 74–75, *75*

shorthand for, 74, *74*
take sheet and, 69
templates and, 67, 93
tempo and, 90
track documentation and, 73, *73*
Track Monitor function on, 27
Transposition function on, 34
direct injection box (DI), *21*, 21–22
direct input
   acoustic guitar and, 53, 54
   electric guitar and, 56
distortion, 5, 46, 52, 57
documentation, of tracks, 73–74, *74*, 101
drums, 62–63
   loops for, 88, *88*, 90
dynamic microphone, 48, 49, 50
Dynaudio Acoustics monitors, 9

E

Earthworks Piano Bar, 62
editing, 31. *See also* mixing
   automation lanes and, 98–100, *99*
   crossfade in, 107, *108*
   documentation and, 101
   with MIDI, 60, 78, 84
   quantization and, 107
electric guitar
   amplifier and, 53, 55, 56, *56*
   audio interface and, 56
   direct input and, 56
   pedal boards and, 57
electricity
   balanced power unit and, 22–23, *23*
   power conditioner and, 23
   power strips and, 22–23, *23*
EQ, 46, 47, *112*
   mastering and, 120
   mixing and, 110–13, 118

F

feedback, 28
Feist, Jonathan, 102
Fire recording app, 16
Firewire port, 2, 5, 25
Focusrite audio interfaces, 6
frequency range, 8, 48, 110–13, *111*

G

gain staging, 46
Gallimore, Byron, ix
GarageBand recording software, 3, 16, 88
Gefell microphones, 49
Genelec speakers, 9
General MIDI (GM), 82
Gobbler backup service, 3

H

hard drives, 2–3
headphone mixes, *70*
   audio interface and, 71
   board mixes and, 71
   panning for, 71
   wet mix for, 71
headphones, 1, 6–7, 25
   DAW and, 66, 70
   microphone and, 7
headroom, 47
high pass function, 46
Hill, Faith, ix
Hinckley, Michael, *54*, 72

I

input ports, 5, 6
iPhone, xi, 15, 16, 43

J

JBL speakers, 9, 11
Joel, Billy, 35
John, Elton, 35
Juice Goose power strips, 23

K

key, 34–35
keyboard
   audio for, 60
   with MIDI, 59, 60–61
Kontakt virtual instruments, 90
Korg keyboards, 96
KRK speakers, 9, 10

L

laptop. *See* computer
latency
   audio interface and, 6
   definition of, 2
lead sheets, 32
Lightning connectors, 25

limitations
  of home studio, 42–43
  in production, 38
limiter, 47
Logic recording software, 3–4, 61, 88
LoopMash recording app, 16
loops. *See also* mixing
  arpeggiator for, 95–96
  arrangement track and, 94
  arranger keyboard and, 96
  in audio, 85, 94
  auditioning of, 93
  choice of, 85–86
  for drums, 88, *88*
  layering of, 95
  marker track and, 94
  MIDI and, 77, *77*, 85, 87
  mixing and, *91*, 91–92
  software for, 97
  templates and, 93
  tempo and, 90
Lynne, Jeff, 63
lyric chart, 32, 36, 100
lyrics, 34, 44

M

marker track, loops and, 94
Marshall stack, 56
mastering
  compression and, 120
  EQ and, 120
  loudness and, 41, 122
  mastering engineer for, 124
  monitors for, 123
  plug-ins and, 42, 121
  reverb and, 120
  software for, 122–23
  song order and, 123
  tools for, 121, 122
McGraw, Tim, ix
Melodyne pitch correction, 106
metadata, 42, 123
microphone, x, 1, 5, 25, 49, 57–58
  acoustic guitar and, 54–55
  boom stand for, 19
  diaphragm in, 48, 50
  headphones and, 7
  level of, 26
  overdubbing and, 105
  pads for, *20*, 20–21

phantom power and, 26, 48
phase and, 47
recording devices and, 15
rental of, 51
schematics of, 51
simple stand for, 19
studio space and, 13
suspension cage for, 19
tracking and, 35, 45–52
troubleshooting and, 29
types of, 48–50
USB port and, 5
MIDI. *See* Musical Instrument Digital Interface
mid-level instrumentation, in mixing, 41
Millennia direct injection boxes, 22
mixdown, 28. *See also* mastering
mixing, 31, 57, 108. *See also* editing; headphone mixes;
    loops; submixes
  DAW and, 66, *91*, 91–92
  EQ and, 110–13, 118
  with loops, *91*, 91–92
  mid-level instrumentation in, 41
  mixing board for, *109*
  pitch correction and, 106–7
  spectrums in, 40–41
  stray sounds and, 105
  T-Pain effect and, 106
  track documentation and, 101
  for vocals, 109
Mogami cables, 19
monitors, 8–10, 25, 27
  flat response and, 8
  for mastering, 123
  panning and, 8
  reverb and, 8
  troubleshooting and, 29
Monster cables, 17
multitrack app, 16
Musical Instrument Digital Interface, 4, 5, 28, 34,
    76–84
  controller for, 81–82
  DAW and, 66, 77, *77*, 85, 87
  editing with, 60, 78, 84
  files for, 76, 78, 87
  interface for, 82, *82*
  with keyboard, 59, 60–61
  loops and, 77, *77*, 85, 87
  quantization with, 60
  virtual instruments track and, 80–81
M-Works Mastering Studios, *124*

N

Neal, Robert, *24*, *59*
Neumann microphone, 49
noise control, 15
Noise Track cable connectors, 17

O

outboard gear, *4*
output bus, on DAW, 28
overdubbing, 36, 45, 101–2
  for corrections, 105
  microphone and, 105
  multiple takes and, 102

P

panning, 110, *113*, 113–14, 118
  for headphone mixes, 71
  monitors and, 8
  templates and, 114
parametric EQ, 121
parametric EQ plug-in, 112
pedal boards, for electric guitar, 57
phantom power, microphone and, 26, 48
phase, microphone and, 47
piano, 61–62
PianoMic mic pads, 21
pitch correction, mixing and, 106–7
plug-ins, 42, 56, 114, *114*, *115*
  for Cubase, 114, *114*, 115, *115*
  mastering and, 121
pop filter, 19–20, *20*
  vocals and, 52
portable recording devices, 15–16
  microphone inputs and, 15
postproduction, 30, 40–42
power conditioner, electricity and, 23
power strip
  electricity and, 22–23, *23*
  voltage meter on, 23
preproduction, 30–33
PreSonus microphone inputs, 15
privacy, of home, xi
production, 30, 33, 37–40
  communications in, 39
  limitations of, 38
  mindset for, 42–44
  psychology and, 39, 40
Propellerhead virtual instruments, 90
Pro Tools recording software, 3–4, 61, 88

Q

quantization
  editing and, 107
  with MIDI, 60
Quantum cables, 17

R

Rabb, Johnny, *62*
Radial direct injection boxes, 21, 22
RAM, 2
real-time recording, 77–78
  tempo and, 78
Record Enable button, on DAW, 27, 28
recordings, as archives, xi, 3
Rectools02 recording app, 16
reflective surface, 13–14, 116
reverb, 43, 115–17, *117*, 118
  for drums, 72
  mastering and, 120
  mixing and, 110
  monitors and, 8
ribbon microphone, 48, 49, 50
Riddoch, Jared, *24*
Rihanna, 3, 38
RME audio interface, 6, *6*
Roland keyboards, 96
Roland V-Drums, 63
rough recording. *See* scratch tracks

S

Saffire audio interfaces, 6
sampler, *83*, 83–84
schedule, for recording, 31
scratch tracks, xi, 31, 32, 33–34, 36
scratch vocal, 101
Sennheiser headphones, 7, *7*
separating tracks, 53
Sequel recording software, 3, 88
shaker click tracks, *68*
Shure SM-57 or 58 microphones, 48, 51
signal flow, 46
signal indicator light, 26
simple stand, microphone and, 19
snakes, for cables, 18
Snapchat, 43
snare drum, 63
social media, ix
software, x, 1, 3–4. *See also* Digital Audio Workstation
songwriter, xii
  audience and, 37
  recording modes of, 25

Sonnox Oxford mastering software, 122
Sony headphones, 7
Sony loop library, 90
Sony recorders, 15
Sony Sound Forge mastering software, 123
Soundcraft cable connectors, 17
sound pressure level (SPL), 48, 49
soundproof rooms, 6, 15
soundscapes, 30, 119
speakers, 11. *See also* monitors
spectrometer, 11, 113
SPL meter, 11
Steinberg Sequel, 3
Steinberg WaveLab mastering software, 123
Steinberg VST Amp Rack, *56*
step-time recording, 77, 78
stereo master track. *See* mixdown
studio space
   acoustic properties of, 11–13, *14*, 64–65
   microphone and, 13
   noise control and, 15
   setup of, 13
submixes, *72*, 72–73
subwoofer, 9
suspension cage, for microphone, 19
sweepable frequency, 112
synthesizer, *83*, 83–84

T

tablet controls, *16*
take sheet
   DAW and, 69
   overdubbing and, 102
Tannoy speakers, 10, *10*, 11
technology, advances in, ix, x
templates
   for DAW, 67
   loops and, 93
   panning and, 114
tempo, 33, 34, 37
   click tracks and, 69
   loops and, 90
   real-time recording and, 78
T-Pain effect, mixing and, 106
tracking, 35–36
Track Monitor function, on DAW, 27
Transposition function, on DAW, 34
Triad-Orbit microphone stands, 19
troubleshooting
   audio interface, 29
   microphone and, 29
   monitors and, 29

U

unbalanced cables, 17
USB port, 2
   audio interface and, 5, 25
   microphone with, 5

V

Varga, Kenny, 10
video, 43
virtual bands, 36
virtual instrument rack, *80*
Virtual Studio Technology (VST) virtual instruments,
   4, 61
vocal riding, 118
vocals
   comping tracks and, 53
   mixing for, 109
   pop filter and, 52
   separating tracks and, 53
   singer placement and, 51–52
   tracking and, 35
vocal up version, 44
voltage meter, on power strip, 23
VST. *See* Virtual Studio Technology

W

waveforms, 27, *27*
Waves mastering software, 122
White, Jack, 32
Wi-Fi, 16
Wolf, Erik, 124
woofer, 8, 9, 10
Wyner, Jonathan, 124

X

XLR cables, 15

Y

Yamaha keyboards, 96
YouTube, 43

Z

Zaolla cables, 17, 19
Zip file, 3
Zoom recorders, 15

0316